OMG

OMG

Growing Our God Images

Mary Ellen Ashcroft

FOREWORD BY Terese Lewis

 CASCADE *Books* · Eugene, Oregon

OMG
Growing Our God Images

Copyright © 2018 Mary Ellen Ashcroft. All rights reserved. Except for brief quotations in critical publications or reviews, no part of this book may be reproduced in any manner without prior written permission from the publisher. Write: Permissions, Wipf and Stock Publishers, 199 W. 8th Ave., Suite 3, Eugene, OR 97401.

Cascade Books
An Imprint of Wipf and Stock Publishers
199 W. 8th Ave., Suite 3
Eugene, OR 97401

www.wipfandstock.com

PAPERBACK ISBN: 978-1-5326-4531-0
HARDCOVER ISBN: 978-1-5326-4532-7
EBOOK ISBN: 978-1-5326-4533-4

Cataloguing-in-Publication data:

Names: Ashcroft, Mary Ellen.
Title: OMG : growing our god images / Mary Ellen Ashcroft. / Cover art by Lisa Palchick.
Description: Eugene, OR: Cascade Books, 2018 | Includes bibliographical references.
Identifiers: ISBN 978-1-5326-4531-0 (paperback) | ISBN 978-1-5326-4532-7 (hardcover) | ISBN 978-1-5326-4533-4 (ebook)
Subjects: LCSH: Metaphor. | Concepts. | Truth.
Classification: P106 .A85 2018 (print) | P106 (ebook)

Manufactured in the U.S.A.   DECEMBER 5, 2018

For my beloved Steve (1978-2015)
in gratitude for all you taught me about life and love.

If you feel you have understood God,
what you have understood is not God.

—ST. AUGUSTINE OF HIPPO

Whether they are pictures and statues outside the mind or imaginative constructions within it . . . images of the Holy easily become holy images—sacrosanct.

My idea of God is not a divine idea. It has to be shattered time after time. God shatters it Himself. God is the great iconoclast.

Could we not almost say this this shattering is one of the marks of God's presence? All reality is iconoclastic.

—C. S. LEWIS, *A GRIEF OBSERVED.*

Atheism has often been a transitional state: thus Jews, Christians, and Muslims were all called "atheists" by their contemporaries because they had adopted a revolutionary notion of divinity and transcendence. Is modern atheism a similar denial of a "God" which is no longer adequate to the problems of our time?

—KAREN ARMSTRONG, *A HISTORY OF GOD*

Contents

Contents

Foreword

"WHAT DO WE TELL the children?" Mary Ellen Ashcroft asked during the first meeting of Deepening Roots, a course she developed to help "grow theologians." Mary Ellen's question captivated me. I had signed up for her class because I could no longer keep up the uneasy truce I had hammered out between the God of my fundamentalist Christian childhood and the God of my liberal Christian adulthood. In my conversion from one piety to another, I had glossed over some essential questions about scripture. The Bible of my childhood and youth was created from whole cloth and handed down from God's lips to my ears through a mysterious process of divine dictation. Never mind exactly how that happened; the unlikely persistence of holy writ through eons of human hostility was evidence of its special magic and its claims over my life. Imagine my surprise when my first religion professor divulged that what I knew as the singular Christian Bible was not one book but many—an entire library of diverse authors and genres, its origins scattered in time and place yet held together in beautiful tension.

In the years since I had left fundamentalism, I had grown more or less comfortable with the notion that in my adoptive faith, the Episcopal Church, we don't take all scripture literally, but we do take it seriously. We read it every Sunday from the lectern, discuss it in rigorous bible studies, and even grapple with its application to our everyday lives. In all that serious thinking, though, I had never been invited to imagine, as we did in the Deepening Roots class, what it might have been like to sit around a campfire as exiles in Babylon—homesick and struggling to understand our experiences as a people of both promise and captivity, heartache and hope, and reshape the story of God's faithfulness to pass along to our children and grandchildren.

I probably didn't look like someone in exile. I was deeply engaged in ministry with children, youth, and families in the same beloved church where my own three children were baptized and nurtured in faith. It was literally my job to figure out what—and how—we would tell the children about God and God's people. But like the displaced children of Israel, I had experienced a lifetime of disorienting and reorienting events, and my theology was fractured and fragmented. Mary Ellen's question struck a deep chord and went to the heart of my work, both professional and personal. What would I tell the children?

What we tell the children who grow up in our church is a world away from the stories of my childhood. I grew up in Sunday schools that were robust and bristling with content. There were flannel boards, worksheets, and prize boxes filled with Jesus-shaped night-lights and glow-in-the-dark praying hands. The Jesus on the wall, with his gentle eyes and wavy hair, looked meek and friendly as he knocked on the door and waited patiently for admission to my heart. But we sang martial songs about putting on the whole armor of God and we practiced "sword drills," racing through our Bibles, vying to be first to leap on top of the table and hoist our Bibles aloft to claim a prize.

My own children began their Christian education in Godly Play, a method of formation that grows from the assumption that children have an innate sense of God's presence, and they lack only the vocabulary to talk about their spiritual experiences. My first experience of Godly Play was a shock. Outside in the hallway, the children took long, slow breaths, quieting their bodies before they tiptoed into the sacred space and formed a ring in front of the classroom altar. They drew languid circles in the sand of the "desert box," shaping and re-shaping the biblical landscape with their fingers. The story was followed by a time of wondering together: *"I wonder which part of the story you liked best? I wonder which part of the story is about you? I wonder if any parts of the story could be left out, and we'd still have all the story we need?"* During response time there were no worksheets to color or paper Bible heroes to cut out with plastic scissors. My children danced the wooden story figures through the desert box, added blasphemous plot twists to the stories, painted vivid pictures that had nothing whatsoever to do with the lesson, at least as far as I could see.

When I began training as a Godly Play teacher, my inner fundamentalist quailed at the loosey-goosey New Age notion that our most important charge was to "wonder together" about the stories. Where was the rigorous content? What about memory verses? And the pace was so slow—we could cover, at most, two dozen stories over the course of a year, and then the cycle began all over again. It took weeks to tell the full story of Abraham and Sarah. Instead of reading the stories authoritatively out of a Bible, we had to tell them from memory. I practiced telling the lessons over and over, beset by nerves as I rehearsed the stories and movements on Saturday nights. What if I got a phrase wrong, or knocked over a figure, and the children giggled or missed the point I was supposed to transmit? Strangest of all, we were discouraged from making eye contact with the children while we told the story. Our eyes were to remain fixed on the story in the center of the circle.

What I discovered as I began to take the Godly Play methods to heart is that the children's eyes were fixed there, too—not on me, or on my imperfect delivery, but on the story between us. Narrative meaning, as Godly Play founder Jerome Berryman explains, is the co-creation of the teller and the hearer, a relational way of knowing that is collaborative and spontaneous. The wondering questions—which felt awkward at first—were essential to the theological work we were doing together. Who is God? What is God like? What do the stories of God's people mean for us? We each had a piece of the puzzle to contribute.

There's a sneaky exercise I like to do with our middle school youth groups. Many come to class wary of God talk, newly agnostic in their approach to faith and struggling to reconcile the religious vocabulary they have grown up with and the disenchanted context they are immersed in Monday through Saturday. The same kids who grew up in Godly Play, mesmerized by the figures moving through the desert box, have absorbed alternative and even hostile messages from our wider culture—messages about who God is and how we talk about Him (and it's almost always Him). Many students bring with them a prefabricated God, a straw man they have fashioned out of their ambivalence as they struggle in the tension between faith and rationality. Early in the year, I lay out dozens of cards on our classroom table, face down. I invite students to choose a card and turn it over. On each is written a word: lion, river, hen, cup, fire, joker, tree, knitter, fortress, fountain, mother, silence, potter, shepherd, king . . . and for each word we do some free associating, jotting down a few adjectives that might describe these things. It begins to dawn on one or two kids that what these words have in common is that they are all metaphors used in the Bible to describe God. Our tabletop is full of words, and yet we have glimpsed only a fraction of who God might be.

Theological card tricks and poetic exercises are good fodder for youth group discussions, but it's hard to have a relationship with a metaphor. What do we do when we crave a more substantial, definitive God, a God whose actions can be predicted and relied upon? For the first decade or so of my adult life, I felt little need for theology. I was carried along in my faith by a new way of worship and by the beauty I found in the Book of Common Prayer. The object of that worship, the recipient of those prayers, was an abstraction to me, until the world tilted one October day and heaved me, quite against my will, into a new story. Our second son, Charlie, was born four months too soon. His one-pound body collapsed after a few days in the NICU, overwhelmed by an infection that couldn't be cured. His primary nurse stood over him for hours, gently inflating his tissue-paper lungs when the mechanical ventilator threatened to shred them. His doctors were grim. "He's very sick," they said, and we tried to decode what that meant for a baby whose grasp on life had been tenuous from the start. "We've done everything we can to support him. The rest is up to Charlie." *Prepare yourselves,* they meant. For days Charlie hung between life and death . . . and then he turned a corner.

Charlie's survival against all odds became, for some of our family members, a testament to God's faithfulness and favor. Theirs was a fierce and muscular Christianity; they talked with bravado about prayer warriors bombarding heaven's gates, and they exulted in every sign that God was at work, healing Charlie's fragile body. But the "miracle baby" narrative made me queasy. What about the full-term baby in the isolette next door, beautiful Lilia with the rosebud mouth and dimpled elbows, languishing from some unknown malady while her doctors worked feverishly to find answers? Were her family's prayers weaker than ours? When Lilia died a few hours after her family took her home, where was the fault? A God who spared some babies—even my own—while dooming others was a God I wanted no part of. And yet I prayed. The NICU nurses plucked my son out of his isolette and tucked him beneath my hospital gown where he curled warm and soft against my chest, no larger than a kitten, and my every breath was a prayer. "Please," I said, in sighs too deep for words, "please." In four months, we brought him home.

A few years down the road, the world tilted again, and our miracle baby ran out of miracles. In a plot twist too cruel for fiction, Charlie was diagnosed with a rare childhood liver cancer. In four months, on another October day, he was gone. In Lifetime movies, this is the part where grieving parents shake their fists and rail at God. But I could find no anger to vent. Faced with a choice between a God who was either capricious or impotent, I chose neither. I wrote a eulogy filled with gratitude for the four years we had with our son, and I meant it. My God was thoroughly bifurcated. There was the God who comforted, and the God who caused. The first God I rested in, the second I denied, pushed back and held out at arm's length to deal with later, if ever.

As the first anniversary of Charlie's death approached, my husband and I were able to go away together, alone. We traveled for the first time to the Canadian Rockies and it was there that God met me again. In the Valley of the Ten Peaks, the sacred silence of the mountains rising in the chill air above the impossible turquoise of Moraine Lake told me all I needed to know of God, for the time being. It was a moment of such purity and awe that I can still feel the sweet ache of it, years later. I felt like Job when, at the end of all his questions, God answers him with a backstage tour of creation. I experienced again the God who is both immanent and transcendent, farther beyond me than the scope of my imagination can ever reach, and yet closer than my next breath. I understood, at last, that the gods I have carried are so much smaller than the God who has carried me.

The pages that follow are an invitation into a deep and rewarding conversation, a chance to examine and retell your stories in a new and compassionate light. As you trace the divine threads that are woven throughout, allow your inner theologian to enlarge and grapple with new insights. Jesus tells us that unless a seed of grain falls to the ground and dies, it cannot grow. We can cling, alone, to god-images that provide little nourishment, or we can let go of our seeds, join them with others, dig them into the soil of our lives, and let the plow churn through. An abundant harvest awaits. As you encounter Mary Ellen's stories and contemplate her questions, let your God grow and stretch and even surprise you. May your own stories speak.

—Terese Lewis

PART ONE

1

Retelling Our Stories in the Light of Our Life Experience and the Biblical Narrative

FOR YEARS I BELIEVED in a magical god who would keep me safe and happy. How comforting this false narrative—despite the fact that it lied to me and (even worse) missed the point. I know now that my (and anyone's) life consists in allowing the inevitable joys and sorrows to reshape me, my life story, and my sense of god. This side of the grave I will never see clearly, "beholding the glory with unveiled face,"[1] but I can cooperate with god as I grope toward greater clarity and authenticity, allowing my story (and thus my god) to be stretched, shattered, and reformed. Over the years my god has morphed from a Santa (who rewarded my good behavior) to one who offers love, grace, and glimmers of presence: a collaborative, "all-shall-be-well" god.

Key thresholds in our lives push us beyond what we believed to be true about ourselves, our families and friends, our place in the world, and our god. We are tempted to put our heads down and cling to the god we have, or to drop that idol, moving on god-less. Instead the divine invites us to release our neat stories and our malleable gods: to allow a new god image to create us.

In literary and biblical studies, and in faith formation work, I have found the insights of narrative theology profound. People have always told stories to remind them of their life orientation, but especially in times when new or contradictory evidence is introduced, people are forced to rethink and retell the old stories.

1. 2 Corinthians 3:18.

Our god images form part of our story, and our narratives shape who we are in the world. "Story" is simple (according to E. M. Forster in his lectures *Aspects of the Novel*). It is the page-turning aspect of a narrative—we ask the question, "What happens next?" Many fairy tales and cheap romances function at this level—we flip through the pages to find out the ending, and then drop the book, not worrying about the characters and how they've grown.

"Plot," according to Forster, goes beyond "story": it looks at the whys. As the narrative unfolds (in memoir or fiction) we meet characters who are grappling with circumstances, losses, challenges—with life. When we engage at the level of plot, we ask how circumstances affect characters, wonder how the character has grown to meet the next challenge in a more integrated way. "Please, Emma," we say to Jane Austen's heroine, "Don't assume you know everything!" Or "Come on, Frodo you can accept help!"

In our own lives, we begin to see that events not only happen to characters, but form them, as the plot thickens. A three-dimensional character, according to Forster, has a past that has led to this present, and is heading toward a future: a unity we sense in ourselves. This character can, as Forster puts it, "surprise in a convincing way"[2]—within this unity of self, the subject has the freedom to do something new or unexpected, but which (upon reflection) fits with what we know of the character.

One character (acknowledged or not) in our stories is the divine, who may don many guises, depending on what we've been taught, what we fear, what we need.

Retelling stories in response to life's traumas is necessary not only for individuals but for peoples. What we call the Old Testament was hammered out during the Babylonian exile, as the children of Israel tried to understand what had happened to them.[3] "God promised us the land as a pledge of our special calling as his chosen people—what are we doing in a foreign city? We had a beautiful temple: how do we understand and tell the story of a faithful god here and now? If we're going to go on living this story, we have got to shape a narrative to pass on to the children."

I imagine these old men, going through their stories, highlighting parts that made meaning of their present situation—ones that show a god who judges disobedience but is ultimately faithful to his promises. This traumatic time of exile—when the very foundations of their lives had

2. Forster, *Aspects of the Novel*, 76.

3. Brueggemann, *An Introduction to the Old Testament*.

broken apart under their feet—was the crucible in which the sacred texts were told, selected, and shaped, with a clear intention: "How do we understand the past in light of the present, and the present in light of the past? What do we want to pass on to the children about what this god is like? About how we practice our faith?" There's a sifting, sorting, molding, and retelling of the story during a time of disruption. (This process, which some may fear lessens the authority of the Word handed down from on high, actually underlines the more profound theological tenet of God's respect for, and collaboration with, humankind.)

A challenging narrative—like the biblical one—provides an overarching story of faithfulness and covenant within the reality of life's struggles. Those who framed the Old Testament included not only the good parts—deliverance at the Red Sea, David slaying Goliath, Daniel in the lion's den—but also the chosen people in the wilderness whining for garlic and David's sin against Uriah and Bathsheba. In that inclusion, they provide us with the bigger story—the cosmic story—of a god who enters into covenant with people, who dialogues with them, who does not shrug off or turn a blind eye to their disobedience, but who is always willing to renew the promise.

The New Testament writings were also shaped in response to cataclysmic disruption.[4] Some good Jews experienced the risen Christ and the Spirit in such a compelling way that they were forced to go back to their sources (the Old Testament) and reshape (past, present, and future) in the light of new evidence. "We thought the Messiah was going to come and defeat the Romans . . ." "How could someone who is so powerful die on a cross?" "How does our monotheistic understanding of God fit with our experience of Jesus and the Spirit?" "How do the law and the sacrificial system (instituted by God) fit with grace?" "Who is this message for?" Once again, god's people must ponder, remember, and reshape the story, so that what is crucial can be passed on. "How do we understand the past in light of the present, and the present in light of the past? What do we want to pass on to the children about what this god is like? About our faith?"

Big, communal narratives must be reshaped: so must our personal ones. In many/most/all lives, a time comes when our narrative fails us. For years the story can be stretched to incorporate new evidence. Our longing to keep the comforting, oft-told tale and our familiar gods seduce us to turn a blind eye to contradictions and inconsistencies. Exile to a strange land, perplexing religious experience: whatever forces us from the fairy-tale is

4. Johnson, *The Writings of the New Testament.*

a gift—often well disguised! The gift forces us to become active shapers of our stories, asking and answering the same questions as those who shaped the biblical canon: "How do we understand the past in light of the present, and the present in light of the past? What do we want to pass on to the children?"

To explore this narrative shaping, this growth in god images, I use parts of my own life narrative. I invite you into my story, joining my reflections on the god I needed at various times of life, along with reflections from narrative theology. I trust that you, looking over my shoulder, will see thresholds in your own life, times you've had to shift your narrative and your god. At the end of the book I offer questions for your reflection— alone, with a spiritual director, or with a small group.

I begin with a key moment in my life. I had no idea it was a key moment: I thought it an annoyance. We all have these thresholds whose profundity is invisible to us at the time. But on reflection: "Oh . . . yes . . . that's when things began to change." These are times (we see in retrospect) that the narrative we've told ourselves about who we are, what the world is like, and who god is, begins to stretch. New information, meekly or boisterously, moves on stage; an old story whimpers its last; a comforting idol feels cold. The story has to be retold in a new way.

2

God Is

WE CONCEIVE OUR GODS. *New Yorker* cartoons, stained-glass impressions from church, overheard conversations, catechism classes, hymns—all these provide god images—ranging from weird to somewhat helpful, though they all, as St. Augustine suggests, are imperfect, subject to our human limitations.[1]

Yes, my god images reveal as much about me as they do about god.

And yet. My limited ability to comprehend god doesn't mean god is not, or even that god is distant or aloof. Despite my lack of maturity/imagination/theological understanding/openness—one thing is clear—god is seeking, wooing, calling.

Often patient and courteous, yet sometimes god seems eager, almost pushy: willing to squeeze through an unexpected opening. My conversion was like that.

I didn't choose where and how to meet god. Perhaps none of us do.

May 1970. My boyfriend promised a friend we'd go hear a speaker at a Presbyterian church. It's a beautiful evening and I don't want to go inside.

Okay, for a bit, just to say hi. Go in but be ready to leave. I'm disgruntled. I sit on an ugly carpet in the Fireside Room, dedicated to the memory of some upstanding Presbyterian. Frowning, arguing over who was predestined for salvation, what would he have made of these long-haired hippies talking about being "high on Jesus"? Maybe, believing in God's ultimate transcendence, he would have sat cross-legged with us. All I knew, as more people filled the room, was that I was beginning to feel claustrophobic: how we were going to get out?

1. Augustine, *Confessions*, 46.

I wore my faded T-shirt and Levis every day. My butt in them on that green shag carpet. What garb could be less appropriate epiphany attire? What decor less conducive to mystical experience? Why not white robes, sunbeams pouring down, a full arched rainbow? Or at least decent aesthetics—marble or mahogany, a cluster of candles and icons in low light? My boyfriend and I had just come in from having sex in the back seat of his father's car, which at least had leather seats.

I don't remember what they spoke about, probably the familiar template, lives sunk in sin before meeting Jesus: "If anyone wants us to pray with them . . ."

How would my life been different had I been nearer to the door, able to stumble out of the room? That moment—that "not escaping"—will become the most profound moment in my life.

I raise my hand. It seemed to me I am saying, can I leave now? I need some fresh air. Can I go to the bathroom?

Called, (fated?), known, (predestined?), someone saw my hand. Perhaps god, (in her infinite mercy and good humor) took my request to go to the ladies' room as a resounding "yes" to a life of faith, and that "yes" has echoed through the years of my life.

Slow motion, as they turn and lay hands on me. "Yes, Jesus we really just pray . . ." "Holy Spirit, fill your daughter . . ." "We claim the blood . . ." Primitive, meaningless incantations: I might have been whirling with dervishes half a world away. But warmth, light, joy rush over me, around me, through me. I'm under a warm waterfall of god.

I turned to Christ and he "saved a wretch like me." For a few years I thought I had raised my hand to accept Jesus as my personal lord and savior. Done him a favor, like saying, "Okay, Jesus, I will go to the prom with you. (Though you'll need to do something about that beard.)"

In a god-haunted world, that moment is nothing and everything. I can disdain bad religious art, dreadful praise choruses, ugly Fireside Rooms, but my perspective is inherently so limited—my enlightened aesthetics evaporate as I meet the divine. My hand reaches up on that May evening, and that movement becomes more life-altering and life-giving than decisions I would later make to move to other continents, get married, have children, get a PhD, get ordained.

That May evening my hand reached up and another clasped it, pulling me from pleasure in the back seat to life wild and unknown. I had no idea I was letting go of a narrow strip between the Cascade Mountains and Puget

Sound forever. Yes, I say, raising my hand toward mystery, I will be born again. The God who touched me that evening has never let me go.

"Do you turn to Jesus Christ and accept him as your Savior?" *The Book of Common Prayer* asks before baptism.[2] Fundamentalism in its literality and individuality tells the story one way—my turning, my accepting. Calvinism tells it another way—God choosing, predestining. Neither encompasses the mystery. That evening I have no idea what I'm getting myself into. I am there and yes, I turn. But it was one of many turns.

2. *Book of Common Prayer*, 302.

3

A Sensual God

WHEN I ACCEPTED JESUS Christ as my personal lord and savior, I stepped from quicksand onto solid ground. The story I told was one of reversal—I had wandered deep in sin, indulging in the pleasures of the flesh, serving the devil, and then wonder of wonders: I was delivered to follow Jesus.

Years later I began to see that coming to Jesus wasn't a u-turn: rather I'd been given a way to name and embrace the giver of life. This life-giver already wooed me, leading me from scarcity to joy through alpine meadows, physical love, and the Milky Way.

Being delivered from a terrible childhood god—one I desperately tried to placate by sacrifice and ritual—toward a sensual god was a move toward grace. The god of sensuality had exorcized the horrors of the other god.

✝

By fourteen I'd stopped going to church with my parents, but I didn't miss the youth group camping trip to Lummi Island, sleeping under the stars with my boyfriend. The youth leader, Bill, spoke to me one evening, voice trembling, "Mary Ellen, you are a leader, for good or evil, and you are hurting this group, encouraging them to have sex. You need to come to Jesus. Are you willing to pray the prayer?"

Bill's eyes were blind to the conversion I'd already had: he couldn't see that he should have hallelujah-ed my life in flesh as blessed deliverance. Glory to God, I'd gone from fearful scarcity, from pastel carefulness, to exuberant pleasures of the body. Praise Jesus! Racing down North Face at Mt.

Baker, hiking along the meadows of Skyline Divide, skinny dipping in the luminaria at Larrabee Beach, kissing my boyfriend on the beach: reborn, I wanted to live!

Sensuality had become my deliverer: claustrophobic within the tiny circle of tepid niceness, I broke through to joy. Walking for miles on tide flats, birds crying, firm sand ripples beneath my feet, picking tiny wild blackberries in ditches on Lummi Island, hiking alongside glaciers, slicing down a slope, sun rosy-ing the mountain tops. And the pleasures of the body, nakedness, diving into icy Puget Sound to see what was growing under Stacia Island's wooden dock.

I laugh out loud when I lower myself into my parents' aqua bathtub . . . I've spent the last couple days on the Heliotrope trail near Mt. Baker. The night sky, my boyfriend's warm body, alpine meadows in full blossom, tiny streams crystal-ing their way over greenest moss, as we moved naked from one joy to the next. My behind was sunburned!

I didn't know it at the time, but I was following in the footsteps of my grandmother, Anna, who died at nineteen. Years later I am going through a trunk with my mom, preparing her to move into assisted living. She pulls out a silver tray, "Would you use this?" she asks.

"No."

"What about these linens? They were my mother's . . ."

"Sure," I say.

Back in Minneapolis, I unfold a large linen table cloth, clearly never used. I pick up a piece with the same pattern and puzzle over it. Twenty feet long and maybe a foot wide. I turn it this way and that.

Then I laugh out loud. Napkins, that Anna ought to have cut apart and neatly hemmed. Instead in her short life, she walked along the river with Conrad and felt her baby kicking.

I laugh and cry over those linens. Anna taught a lesson polar opposite to the one I'd been taught by her daughter, my mother: work first, then pleasure.

My mother was terrified of the flesh. And who could blame her? Anna—who had not hemmed those napkins, whose warm milk and smooth flesh touched hers—turned cold and then to dust.

The sensual god, the giver of all good gifts, delivered me, yet I was dizzied by freedom.

I went into that Fireside Room believing I was free; years later I could see my desperation. Like many who find shelter in fundamentalism, I needed a haven from anxiety and uncertainty. The mystery that encompassed me that May evening provided a clear structure: relying on the clarity of the Bible, I would be safe. I wouldn't be the first or last to claim certain texts in response to a scary diagnosis, a financial crisis, even the confusing mixture of people in the supermarket.

Like the children of Israel, disturbed that their leader has been up the mountain in a cloud, I needed some firm foundation to my life, because my 1970 world was spinning out of control.

I lied to my parents to sneak out with my boyfriend, lied to one boyfriend to be with another. I lied to a doctor to put myself on the pill, while one of my friends went to a "home" in Seattle to have her baby, the other to Vancouver to have an abortion.

I lean into floor cushions at my friend Lisa's house, her dad's *Playboy* magazines stacked on the floor and nude photographs of her mom on the walls. We listen to *Hair* and giggle about masturbation.

My brother comes back from Vietnam, carrying wads of cash from dealing drugs. We skip school and smoke pot. Jill and Lisa blow their minds on bad acid trips. We drive too fast, passing on curves, up to Mt. Baker.

The world was quicksand. I wasn't sure how long I would survive. I needed a new god to hold me firm.

4

A God Who Is Out to Get You

I FLED TO THIS sensual god to break away from my fearsome childhood deities. Those early gods—from family or church—may be cumbersome, even terrifying. Dropping this haunt—one glimpsed in a bloody crucifix, heard in a hollered sermon, or one who like mine was homegrown—can be a deliverance. Mine had been shaped over years.

⊕

Look with me at this family portrait, Yakima, 1955: big brother Kent, his six-year-old hand resting manfully on his knee. Baby Bruce, smiling impishly. My legs tucked sideways, a starred Band-Aid on my knee. In the family cast, Kent played the mischievous one, Bruce starred as baby, while I was endearing.

Near the family portrait one other face catches my eye: a faded sepia photo of mysterious Grandma Anna who died of diphtheria less than a month after my mother was born. Her smile so joyous: I wonder, would she have loved me? The profound question lurked beyond my childish reach: what would my mother have been like had she not suffered this cosmic loss?

My mother's immense loss, passed to me through her milk, taught me that god was terrible. My best bet was to be invisible, but if I couldn't be that, then I could be sweet.

My first memory, I'm sitting on the rug watching Daddy build a fire. He kneels on the black tiles in front of the fireplace, crumpling a *Yakima Herald*. Daddy presses a stick against his knee and grimaces, his teeth bared like an animal's, and then the wood cracks. He arranges the wood like a tiny teepee, and I hand him the box of matches. The little flame spreads along the paper and begins to crawl up the kindling. Daddy places bigger pieces of wood in an x across the teepee. I stare into the fire. It is a city, like Yakima, and it is being engulfed and blackened by flames. The people who live here, they are all asleep, so they will perish. What have they done to deserve this? Nothing. This is what happens. Tiny figures on top of the sticks hold up their arms to me, pleading. I watch their world crash in destruction. When will this happen, I wonder, to mine?

First Presbyterian was a huge brick church, whose best quality (from what I could see) was its full-sized gym in which we roller skated—crack the whip!—on Saturday afternoons and attended Vacation Bible School in the summer, drinking pixie cups of red Kool-Aid, eating Graham crackers, and playing Red Rover. Near the bathroom hung a picture of a serene and otherworldly Jesus—looking upward, glowing slightly, placid as anything. Even his hair curled in a tranquil kind of way.

This Jesus never made it home, though I would have welcomed one who could calm our fears, who might glow in a stable where "all is calm, all is bright." I couldn't imagine sleeping in heavenly peace.

Yakima, Washington was an apple-growing center, and Sundays in early spring—when tender blossoms had appeared in the orchards and the frost might kill them—we would enter the large sanctuary and see hanging clouds—not from incense but from smudging—the burning of tires in metal pots throughout the orchards.

The god of holy smoke, roller skating, and Kool-Aid had little chance against our home gods. I picture a duel, akin to Elijah pitting the most-high god against the Baals—my home god of scarcity and terror vs. red bricks, Graham crackers, and roller skating. No—the daily sacraments at home showed me which was most powerful.

Meals were sacraments—outward and visible signs—of this god of scarcity. Money was tight—my mom stayed home, and my father had jobs, not a career—keeping the books at Aves Millwork, teaching accounting, typing, and shorthand at the local business college. He shifted to new jobs as easily as he might have changed shirts. Affable, good humored, friendly—I smile to think of him years later on the London Underground, starting up conversations with embarrassed Londoners and then dropping his voice to say, "You know . . . we're Americans . . ."

When my two brothers and I went grocery shopping with my mom, we had already watched as she sat on the couch clipping coupons from the local papers, listing the name of the store and what was on special at Safeway and Albertsons.

Each meal was carefully prepared with what should have been enough food—after all, she'd graduated magna cum laude from the University of Washington in nutrition and home economics at a time when not many women earned degrees. Her aunts, Edie and Flossie, had funded her university education. She knew what a person needed to eat. Each meal was nutritionally balanced, with meat, starch, vegetables, and dessert. Each plate was colorful, with a small scoop of cottage cheese, garnished with a slice of pineapple.

And yet my brothers, father, and I were constantly hungry. The packet of butterscotch pudding—always the kind cooked on top of the stove and not instant!—was rationed into five custard cups. My dad and later my brothers, found ways to appease their appetites elsewhere. Sometimes Dad would come in with a story about how he'd gone out with a colleague after work and they'd stopped somewhere, and he'd ordered lemonade, and behold! It was spiked. When my dad smelled that way it terrified me, since I knew how demonic drink was. Years later when I was twelve—my first babysitting job for some neighbors—I opened their fridge and there was beer! "Are they communists?" I wondered.

My mom gossiped with Mrs. Eitrim and Mrs. Kohler about a new neighbor, who spoke little English. A war bride, from somewhere in Europe, she looked perpetually frightened. Her husband was a grouch, so we wouldn't even step on their property on weekends. But once a week after school I'd say to the neighborhood kids, "Okay, let's go ask Mrs. Smith for a snack." We paraded to her back door. I'd push some of the smaller kids to the front and knock. I'd rehearsed their lines with them, "Mrs. Smith, do you have something to eat?" Poor woman, alone in a strange country with a grumpy husband and no children of her own; she looked at us wide-eyed—did she get in trouble when her husband got home for breaking into the freshly baked cake? I stood at the back trying to look mortified at the egregious behavior of my younger compatriots. She would come back with big slices of orange or spice cake for us—layered cake, not the practical block from a nine-by-thirteen–inch pan. We thanked her profusely and sat on her step devouring this wonder in ecstasy.

It would be years before I realized that this scarcity, this tragic starvation of her family, was an extension of my mom's anorexic self-deprivation. Her loss of her mother—eyes twinkling and mouth twitching with a smile (in an era when pictures were serious moments)—sealed my mother's fate, her way of seeing and being in the world. Her mother's untimely death taught my mother a message that could never be expressed: at a profound level, my mother knew that any good, any abundance was about to be snatched away—and you would be left hollow, rooting for sweet milk, for flesh against flesh, for loving joy. Anna's husband ran into the hills when she died, and I met him only twice, when Conrad had remarried a sensible square-faced woman and lived in a square, red brick house in Spokane. When Conrad died, my mother found a recently scribbled note in his papers, "Please bury me next to Anna." Anna had died fifty years before. My mother threw the paper away.

As a sensitive child I absorbed dread. Mom didn't need to tell me that the world was a horrendous place where anything good and lovely could (and would) be taken away, and where abundance was suspect. Atrocious things happened, and even though we were not allowed to watch programs with war or violence, I knew from the silences when certain subjects were brought up—the doctor who had a brain tumor, the woman from church who had to go see a specialist . . .

Yakima itself, with its dinosaur-foot hills and spreading orchards, might have been lovely, but its extremes—over a hundred in the summer and in the twenties in the winter—meant that my mother saw it as hostile territory. Not as bad as North Dakota where my father had grown up, but not the mild, grey, green slumbering place west of the mountains where she was raised.

We lived near the orchards and often played in them. We were not allowed to pick the apples, pears, or peaches, because these belonged to the owners. "No throwing dirt clods," was one of the rules: children had died from a rock accidently hidden in one. "No playing in the irrigation ditches," which crisscrossed the neighborhoods. We were told tales of errant children, who had hopped into a ditch, just to fetch a ball, exactly when the sluice gates were opened, and those children were never seen again.

I took this in and had night terrors from an early age, terrible dreamlike states: Crushed, flattened, squeezed at the bottom of a well, chill water over under and in me, legs tied, arms bound, mouth stuffed with rags. Head thrashing, mouth opening wider, wider . . . Somehow, I need to count all the rocks, stack them all, or they would crush me, would flatten my mommy. My lungs burst. Legs aching, I find the doorknob.

The cool linoleum of the bathroom floor presses my cheek, "I can't, I can't . . ." I sob.

"What can't you do, Mary Ellen?" my intervenim other asks.

"I can't count them, but I have to and if I don't, if I . . . don't even make me tell you or it will happen . . . and Mommy . . . I would, Mommy really I would if I could, but I can't . . ." I twist. "I wish I was dead. Who can get me out of this? I can't get out of this. I wish I was dead."

"You must never say that," she says. "Les, take her for some fresh air on the porch, and I'll get her some Dramamine."

The cold hits me. "It can never work. Please, let me go, I must at least start . . ." Mommy holds the sticky yellow Dramamine in front of me. "Open," she says, and I swallow it. She pulls me into the house and wipes my forehead and around my mouth with a pink washcloth.

"I can't live like this. It's too terrible. They will win, I know it . . . just let me die."

"I never want to hear you talk that way again. It's just a bad dream. Do you hear me?" She closes my bedroom door.

Years later I began to understand the haunts that followed her as she slipped into bed next to Dad. Oh, Mom. You lay there looking at the ceiling, trying to keep your eyes skinned to ward off your own night terrors, to elude dreaming that cosmic loss of mother: where O where O where O where O where . . . My rooting lips, parched mouth, strangled throat . . . nothing warm . . . starvation . . . Wail, wail . . . no one comes. Sob, whimper. No one can come, no one will come. Haunted . . . pursued . . . possessed . . . Black, black, black . . . I open my mouth . . .

⌘

This terrible god seeped into me through my mother's milk, her set face, her trembling hands. My brothers seemed oblivious, while her terrors framed and permeated my whole world. The best I could do was wear pastel colors and move under the radar by being very, very, very, very nice.

Fear devoured my young life but could never be spoken. The whispers adults used for horrors made that clear. Had I spoken my dread of losing my mother, I'd find her electrocuted on the bathroom floor. Talked about my father's commute and he would have been crushed in a car accident. Confided my horror of thunderstorms—might as well paint a bull's-eye on our house.

Instead: pretend terrible things didn't happen—no sad stories, no war movies. Be careful, quiet. Eat tiny portions, wear soft colors. My mother's life was so straitened, so tiny, so constricted, that I struggled to find a place in it. From early days I would clean—dusting their room, my room—hoping for a place, for praise.

✥

My mother's fear of those wide-open spaces, of the heat and the cold of the plains, of any extremes, cut us off from Dad's family. We lived as if my dad, as well as my mom, was an orphan.

I can see now how my mother's loneliness was typical of homemakers in the fifties, before Betty Friedan's *Feminine Mystique* provided words for her isolation.[1] She and her peers had been convinced that, as wives and mothers, they stood at the pinnacle of life's fulfillment. Societal pressure suspected close friendships, which might threaten that primary closed circuit between husband and wife. My mother had neighbors with whom she chatted, and a couple of others she called friends, but deep sharing went against social norms and her personality.

Where was god? Not in the Presbyterian Church. Not at home, where the prayers before meals were rattled off: "Bless this food to our use and us to thy service. Amen." Before bed, "Now I lay me down to sleep I pray the Lord my soul to keep." We edited out the next part, "if I should die before I wake"—obviously that would be asking for it, pretty much putting up a sign in six-foot letters on top of the house saying, "Meteor strike here." The one who prayed such profligate words would certainly die that very night. Instead I prayed, "God bless mommy and daddy and Kent and Bruce and Edie and Flossie and Nikki and all the chipmunks. Amen." This prayer—"so cute"—was light-years away from my terrors.

Sweetness, niceness, respectability might protect us. I open a new box of crayons, mesmerized by their pungent smell, the parade of cornflower, magenta, forest green. I despise sky blue, pink, primrose, but those were the colors I put inside the lines, light blonde hair swishing, a touch of rose on light "flesh" cheeks. Bright colors were a kind of hubris: I would not admire

1. Friedan, *The Feminine Mystique*.

them in the fabric aisles nor put them in my coloring books. To be notice-
able was to risk the wrath of the gods. Pale was beautiful.

If my mother could choose a favorite picture of herself, I suspect it
would be this one:

She wears her going-away outfit—made in a university textiles
course—highlighting her excellent posture. Grace looks directly at the
camera, pleased with herself for having married this handsome young man.

Les stands next to her, smiling his public smile, uncomfortable in his
double-breasted suit.

Bleak and tired next to the newlyweds, stands Grace's grandfather,
Kent, with his handlebar moustache, old-fashioned suit, rumpled vest,
woolen knees bagged and shiny.

There's no woman in this Everett park to feel proud of Grace, just as
there was no woman to talk to her about sex on her wedding eve. Her two
maiden aunts have helped pay for the wedding. Looking at the camera, she
knows nothing of the messy complications of bodily love.

But one thing she knows. The body is dirty, and sex is about losing control. Dirt and germs are everywhere. Look what happened to her mother.

On our family vacations, Mom was terrified. Not only was every car
coming down the road almost certain to swerve head-on into ours, but
there were other dangers. Food you hadn't prepared! Portions might be too
big!

Terrible germs lurked in motels. To sleep in a bed not your own, sheets
not laundered by you: this was hazardous. She'd say to the owner of a motel
in a shrill voice: "May I look at a room." Not a question. We'd watch from
the back seat of the car for her face as she came out. She would never say,
"It's wonderful." A high score was, "Well, it seems clean." More often she'd
come out, grim faced: "It will do." Or traumatized, she'd look at us and
shake her head very slightly, nostrils pinched, as if she'd seen a ghost, close
the car door, and speak in low tones to my dad.

Flies were dangerous. "Oh Les, a fly." All those germy little footprints
that had been in dog poop (for heaven's sake) were now on the cookies.
Horrible diseases multiplied already.

5

A Magical God

HUMANS—EVEN THE EARLIEST AND most primitive—created ritual to provide an illusion of control. Ritual is central to much religious experience—be they nuanced eucharistic liturgies, a few Hail Marys rattled off, or a chicken sacrificed. Our lives are full of all kinds of rituals—making candy-coated nuts for Christmas, stepping aside to not walk under a ladder, burying a statue of Joseph to sell the house.

Ritual helps us reinforce our stories about god. Annual Passover celebrations or Christmas pageants: these narrate and reenact who god is and what god demands.

I developed rituals to placate this god, and they seemed to work. When my mom decided to renew her teaching licensure in Ellensburg, she drove off in our little Fiat toward the dreaded canyon road. Every morning I made sure I was on my knees on the couch waving to her—maybe then she'd be okay, and that little car would pull into the driveway that evening.

Watching her drive off, pleading I might see her again: did some tiny bit of Sunday school teaching lurk among the gods of fear and scarcity, the trickster god who might catch you smiling and slap you so hard you'd never know what hit you? I don't think so.

Who needs a god whose arm can be twisted by sacrifice and ritual? I did. The church held no god able to meet my fearsome one.

∽

In Yakima Dad worked as an accountant at Ave's Millwork. When the demand for wood doors slowed, he found a business college needing a director in Kennewick. Ninety miles south and east, Kennewick was in the wrong direction—away from the green forests of Western Washington. Plenty of sage brush, scrubby trees, tumbleweeds piled up on fences. Dusty and hot.

My mom was the stable bread winner, but a good woman followed her man's job; for security she kept her teaching job for the next year and my dad drove to Yakima Wednesdays and weekends.

Every Wednesday and Friday we waited, terrified, for the call from the State Patrol informing us, regretfully, that he was dead. Mom's mouth, eyes, and breath all resonated in me like high overtones. We shut the door into the living room where Bruce and Kent were watching TV and moved silently around the kitchen, hoping beyond hope for the miracle: that we'd hear his car pulling into the driveway. One Wednesday he arrived early, so that when I tripped out from choir practice, he was there in the car! I broke down sobbing . . . one day delivered from the terrible terror of waiting.

I still have the Ready Kilowatt cookie cutter we were given on moving into an all-electric house that June. Although the Columbia River flowed nearby, there were no parks or swimming places. Nature consisted of Saturday tours of Columbia River dams with their fish ladders and water hazards at a par three golf course where my brother and I dove for golf balls to sell. We counted cars on freight trains snaking by the house and went to baseball games at the local diamond, smelling hops and mint those summer evenings.

In fifth grade I had nightmares about the Cuban missile crisis. In my dream, everyone in my eastern Washington hometown scrambled onto a huge cardboard box, a uniformed man cranking a wheel to start it. The engine whined and the box-plane bounced a few yards, stuck in the sagebrush. "Look!" a woman shrieked, pointing to missiles screaming over the horizon.

We lived near the Hanford Atomic Plant and I'd heard adults: "If those damn commies press the button, we'll never know what hit us." I walked into town past a hardware store with a galvanized steel igloo out front. "Keep Your Family Safe" read the sign taped to the bomb shelter. My brother laughed as we drove past: "Incinerate your family," he said.

I tried to block the clear images of squatting in there, holding our dog Nikky. I moved toward my destination: the Religious Book and Gift Store. I slipped in, afraid I'd see someone from school. The coast was clear. But what if a clerk approached and asked if she could help me? What if I broke down? Yes, please, I might sob. People pretend everything's okay, but it's not. Please . . .

I tried to look casual as I fingered four tiny books with gold and silver covers. On each page was one inspiring verse containing the word gold or silver. I also bought a card with an amiable looking Jesus and a glow-in-the-dark cross underneath.

At home I taped the cross to the wall above my bed. I tried to memorize three or four verses. I didn't understand them, but that didn't matter. My job was to recite them, like some primitive incantation. I turned out my light, listening for footsteps. I didn't want my mom to see me as I threw off my covers and knelt on my bed. She might think I was afraid. I glowed in the dark at the idea of having to mention my fear to her. If I said it, the horror would happen. Nuclear holocaust, and all my fault.

No footsteps, so I kissed the cross. Its eerie green light traced the line between Jesus and me, its color the same as nuclear fallout, which, like Jesus, would never go away.

If I kept to my part in this ritual, maybe Jesus (or god—I wasn't picky) would do his and keep my world from blowing to smithereens. I was a savage, beating my breast.

⌖

My closest friend Mary was the eldest of twelve children in a two-bedroom house. On the playground we compared god notes, convinced the other was going to hell. She sobbed when Kennedy was shot; I watched television coverage for hours as I babysat the kids next door. Above their couch was a cityscape painting of light dripping into water: it blends forever in my psyche with Jackie's and the children's faces.

The next fall I started junior high— "Highland Scotties, Rah, Rah, Rah!!!" Before school started each morning, the kids walked the halls, checking out who was wearing what and walking with whom. My mom, who taught there, disapproved, so I did too.

I was twelve, and all the girls were begging their moms to buy them nylons to wrinkle on their newly shaven legs, and snapping each other's bras in the hallways. When one of the girls (with matronly bosom and adult odor) cruised toward me to snap my (nonexistent) bra, I spun round, trying to appear nonchalant as my skinny body nearly fell into my locker. Giggle, whisper, "She doesn't?"

The girls' room was the platform of the school, where in-ness and out-ness were measured. Oh, the joy of having a pimple to press in the mirror, while the rest tried out words like "zit," stopping to tease back a few hairs. I slip straight into the stall, hoping every time that I'd find a spot of blood on my underpants, so I could say, "Oh rats, my period's arrived." No spot of blood, I wash my hands and catch a peripheral view of myself in the mirror. If I stop and look at the pin-curled brown hair, the pointy glasses, it might seem that I care. Years later, my six-year-old granddaughter sees a picture of me at this age and turns to me, "Why did you look like that?" "My mom wanted me to." "Oh, Babka!" she laughs.

And then my mother pushed me out of the nest. The Kennewick paper ran a two-inch story about a memorial library dedicated to JFK. I decided to organize a car wash, asked a few friends to help, made posters, put an announcement on the local radio station. We washed and washed and raised 130 dollars!

That evening I climbed into bed, feeling tired, proud, happy.

My mom came in to tuck me in, her mouth rigid. "Mom?" I asked.

"Well, I can't see how that was your business at all . . . asking people for money for something like that . . .

"But Mom . . .," I looked at her face and started to cry. She pursed her lips and left the room.

I sobbed.

I didn't understand, but I knew: I could not please her and have my own life.

Years later, when I had my own children, scenes from my childhood rushed back and I realized her fear crowded out love; she had only enough to lavish on a parade of small dogs.

Where was god that evening she walked out of my bedroom? If I'd had the words I might have wondered what kind of god allowed her loss to be visited on another generation, had permitted my being raised without loving abundance. But the shutting of that door, was the opening of another: she shoved me into freedom.

A few months later, my dad's job ended again, and his new job was in Bellingham. Fishing, crabbing, swimming, beach combing on Puget Sound, hiking, and skiing in the mountains since I could never please my mom, I could turn to the beauty of the world and the joys of the flesh—skin on skin, cool water on body, wind in hair rushing down a hill.

6

Your God Calls You to Come Out from Among Them

AT EIGHTEEN, I HAD never read about stages of moral or spiritual development. But I knew how different my experience of Jesus was from the religion I'd known. First Presbyterian offered nothing potent enough to battle my terrible fears. My childhood religion had let me down, and church seemed like the last place to find a god I craved.

Fortunately, my new god did not attend church. We Jesus People despised the "institutional church": it was like spitting to even say it. The institutional church was the "whore of Babylon" from the book of Revelation. It offered people a vaccine against the real savior, who was coming back any day now. These so-called churches were not "Bible-believing," nor did they offer an intensely personal (but also high and mighty) savior. I knew god could not be found in the church: fortunately, the Jesus People and other fundamentalist groups offered me a home.

A month after my conversion, I graduated from Bellingham High School and started at Western Washington State College. There I became fully immersed in the Jesus People. We met in the college quad and sang choruses over and over: "His banner over me is love . . ." "I wish we'd all been ready . . . children died . . . the days grew cold . . . I wish we'd all been ready . . ." "The steadfast love of the Lord . . ."

We prayed, "Lord we just really ask you . . ." And seven days a week we studied "the wordagod." Our motto: The Bible says it; I believe it; and that settles it. The creation happened in six days—see, it's right here in black and white. We pondered end times prophecy, flipping from Hebrews to Leviticus, Philippians to Isaiah.

This god made everything completely clear. Why couldn't people see the obvious? Jesus was coming again soon, so nothing in the world around me—college classes, hiking in the mountains, biking through town—really mattered. We were engaged in a battle in heavenly places, "not against flesh and blood but against the principalities and powers" (Ephesians 6:12). Our classes were giving us "the wisdom of the world." Which was passing away. Useless.

We were assured that "whatever is not of faith is sin": this covered most of college life. How could writing a paper on Virginia Woolf or understanding *The Brothers Karamazov* make any real difference? If my professor (who I liked so much) was perishing, would spend eternity in hell because I hadn't shared the Four Spiritual Laws with him, how could I even think about the *Aeneid* (or Dante's *Inferno*, for heaven's sake) at such a crucial time?

My greatest love was skiing, but because Jesus was coming soon to judge the world, it was a waste of time and money—unless I evangelized on the chair lift. A couple of times I skied single, schussing toward the chair lift, shouting "single" to clamber on with some poor unsuspecting soul. We looked at Mt. Shuksan: "Did you ever wonder who made all this?" "Nope." A bit later as the chair moved over a deep rocky canyon, "Did you ever think, if you fell off this chair lift, where you would spend eternity?" "Nope." He'd be sorry when the rapture came, and he had to face the Great Tribulation. I stopped skiing.

No time to question: I took classes, worked part time at the Whatcom County Library, went to Bible study every night. Itinerant preachers moved to the area since god had called them to bring us the wordagod. Brother Mel was sent to Bellingham by god who assured him he would have a life built on a foundation of precious stones. When our study was over that first day, we needed to look at the pebbles someone had attached to the concrete stairs of this house they *happened* to rent: See how god keeps his promises? Sometimes the teaching god put on his heart took hours to get through, but it was worth it because we understood god's plan for women to wear long skirts and keep their heads covered. Fundamentalism even provided career planning: I learned I was created to be a wife, or helpmeet as we called it.

After the teaching the women would get up and put food on the table, while the guys in the group discussed end times issues with Brother Mel. Sometimes Brother Mel's wife would bring a timely word to me, "Mary Ellen, this dessert is very good, but a smaller portion would be perfectly adequate."

Jerry had white blond hair, small eyes, and pointy teeth: during Bible study he picked his acne scabs. He cornered me one night: "Mary Ellen, I believe the Lord is calling us to get married." I recoiled, but several of my friends married guys in the group, and because the Bible said we were to be fruitful and multiply, started having baby after baby.

Pressing questions—about other religions, why bad things happen to good people, the environment, women's roles—were ignored. We debated eternal security—if someone was saved and fell away, were they still saved? Was the gift of tongues authentic or only for an earlier dispensation before god's ultimate revelation in Scripture was complete? Or the really big one—were you prelapsarian or postlapsarian in your understanding of what would happen to believers during the Great Tribulation?

After a couple years, members of our group started to "fall away." I knew my time was coming: Sitting in Mr. Wallace's humanities class, loving E. M. Forster and Tolstoy, I began to realize that Mr. Wallace wasn't going to look at my empty chair one day and think, "Maybe she was right. She must have been taken at the rapture. Maybe I should think about the state of my eternal soul, before it's too late."

I felt deeply torn. How could I walk away from the Love who had drenched me that May evening and held me since? But how could Love so boundless demand that I despise literature and mountains?

PART TWO

PART TWO

7

Your God Is Too Small

WHEN CHILDISH GODS BECOME too small to handle life's realities, the choice may seem simple: clutch dogma for "dear life," shutting out questions and quoting Bible verses. Or ditch god altogether. "I no longer believe in god," people say to me.

"Tell me," I say, "about the god you no longer believe in."

"I think I am still holding a god I was given in junior high," a friend tells me. "There was no way for that god to grow." Her life, with its joys, and traumas come, and she clutches a teddy bear god.

Our god images must grow as we do. My seventh-grade god would have sent my best friend Mary to hell for being Catholic—what would he do with the Muslim family who have moved in next door? The cognitive dissonance forces us to discard idols, be they religious or secular (capitalism, self-fulfillment, luxury, or humanism). These relics litter our life journeys, like abandoned rocking chairs or pump organs along the Oregon Trail.

Most of us have read studies tracing human development in terms of intellectual understanding and moral decision-making. My youthful concepts—myself at the center of the world, my patriotism—these must change as I mature, like a simplistic model of the universe, with a grapefruit sun at the center. Most of us look back and chuckle at how, when we fell in love, we knew so clearly that we'd found a love far superior to our parents' romance. Or the way it seemed so obvious how to deal with an obnoxious two-year-old (before that two-year-old was ours). In most areas of understanding, time passes, and cognizant of life's realities (and aware of slippages of language and symbol systems), we see that we've had to shift our seemingly unshakeable ideals.

Many young people I talk to are very sophisticated in their thinking as we discuss novels, movies, world affairs. But their sense of religion or theology is stuck at an elementary school level. No wonder they struggle to let go of their deities, fearing they'll find nothing left and go to hell. Or they drop their idol and move on—proudly atheist. Perhaps, as Karen Armstrong suggests, the atheism of young people today is a recognition of the inadequacy of our old gods within our pluralistic, postmodern world.

Fundamentalism's god was predictable and comforting, since those "everlasting arms" were exceptionally twistable. As long as we asked, "in his name" our prayers were answered. Jesus would keep his promises and keep me from all harm. My arbitrary and terrifying childhood god had been pushed aside, as had the god of those fleeting pleasures of the flesh. I had been delivered from the quicksand of hedonism onto the solid rock of the Bible.

But now my fundamentalist god had me in a bind. Obviously, I couldn't turn toward the "institutional church" since that would be slipping into a state of "lukewarmness," and I knew that in the book of Revelation Jesus warned the church at Laodicea that they were neither hot nor cold—they were lukewarm, and thus Jesus would "spew them out of his mouth." I did not want to be spewed, so I could either remain in fundamentalism, marrying one of the guys and being fruitful and multiplying. Or I could "fall away," but that would mean leaving my social circle, my way of thinking and being in the world, and my god. If I made the wrong choice I might go to hell or have to live through the Great Tribulation (depending on where I stood in terms of being pre-, post-, or intralapsarian). Was it possible for someone who had been saved, to turn away and be saved again? Probably not. You see, I knew my Bible well.

Almost exactly three years after I had accepted Jesus Christ as my personal Lord and Savior, I went to Pete's and heard a recording of the Choir of King's College Cambridge singing *The Service of Nine Lessons and Carols*.

⌘

A voice major at Western, Pete invited me over once or twice a month to listen to a new record. We lit our usual candle, turned out the lights, and lay on the carpet of his parents' living room.

I felt torn and wretched as I lowered myself onto that carpet. Why would god demand I go into a college class afraid I might like it? Didn't he have more on his mind than how much I loved skiing? But I couldn't shake the waterfall of love that had poured over me three years before. Why would god enjoy our repetitious prayers and bad choruses sung ad nauseam? I guess I had to turn away from faith . . .

Then the voices:

Of the Father's Love Begotten, ere the worlds began to be;

He is alpha, from that fountain, all that is and has been flows.

Of the things that are, that have been,

and that future years will see: evermore, and ever more.[1]

My heart rose, like a flame in a séance. Someone had written these words hundreds of years ago. (Similar but different from "In the name of Jesus, in the name of Jesus, we have the victory!!!") A world away in time and space . . .

In the light of one candle I caught a glimpse of a god looming larger than my fundamentalist one. The divine voice echoing through this room had not sprung into existence with Brother Mel or Brother Roger and their teachings from the "wordagod." This god, coming to me from Cambridge, England, would not demand I switch off my brain when I switched on my faith. Maybe this one had created trees and mountains and would not ask me to turn away from them.

These voices, echoing through that fifteenth-century chapel and this twentieth-century living room, warmed my heart with a promise of delight outdoors and in the life of the mind.

When the record finished with a Bach organ piece, I staggered out the door. I was like Lazarus, hopping toward the light as my bandages began to fall. I went to my VW bug and sat. I could no more dispense with god than life. I must follow.

But pursuing this new god . . . How could I stay in Bellingham? I ran into old friends who shook their heads sorrowfully because I'd fallen away. I couldn't begin to explain what had happened to me, how my god was growing.

I decided to take a two-week summer class at Regent College in Vancouver. Hearing lectures on the earliest church and Paul's letters—I felt alive, engaged—like the best hiking I'd ever done. I sunbathed on a nude beach near the UBC campus, reading Berkhof's *Systematic Theology*. I felt

1. *The Hymnal 1982*, #82.

as if I'd fallen in love—with learning, theology, biblical studies—the life of the mind and faith intertwined.

In a dinner line next to the English New Testament professor, flummoxed by his accent, I asked about the seminary he taught at, and he jotted down my name and address. The materials arrived a couple weeks later—mimeographed, with bad type and grainy black and white pictures. How did this fit with the god of lovely descants under a vaulted fan roof at Kings?

I didn't know, but I applied to St. John's Theological College in Nottingham and sold my beloved bicycle to help finance the trip. My great aunt gave me some money. "It's either you or the Impeach Nixon campaign," she said.

I listened to the cassette tape I'd made from Pete's record. I pressed start and the boy sopranos from Kings College (unbeknownst to them) conjured me through passport control into a new world.

8

Goodbye to God and Country

WHEN WE CAN NO longer stretch our stories, they break apart, and a new story must be told. As Alasdair MacIntyre writes, this is true in scientific theories and our life stories.[1] When the paradigm changes (such as the shift to a heliocentric universe), not only must the present narrative shift, but also the past and future. The simple story line—this happened, then this, then that—fails to incorporate all the data. We are larva, growing as much as we can within our crusty bounds: we must split our exoskeleton.

When the story breaks, the god we have fashioned stands in the dock. Birth, illness, cross cultural experience, divorce: any of these may trigger a crumbling of certainty. We look at the god we're clutching and see an idol—not deserving our obedience or worship. The god who would answer every prayer: it's not so simple. We could hunker down, clutch our idol to our chests . . .

God's evolution is no new plot line. Scripture tells stories of people gripping their idols, afraid to grow into a bigger god. When Moses goes up the mountain, the people decide god is dead and make a golden calf. They don't really want debauchery (as Cecil B. DeMille would have it) but the good old days when they had gods they could see, touch, and manipulate.

There in Pete's living room, I had been bewitched, sung toward a place where history crisscrossed beauty, voices soared into high clerestory spaces, where the split I'd endured between faith and self would not be countenanced. I had played that little tape over and over as the rumbling pipe organ and piping descants promised a weaving together of experience

1. MacIntyre, "Epistemological Crises, Dramatic Narrative, and the Philosophy of Science."

and intellect, tradition and newness, art and reality, things earthly and heavenly. Maybe in this new place, I could pursue a god who called toward integration rather than division.

I couldn't see then that this new conversion would not only deliver me to an English seminary, but also lead me to the flora, fauna, and people of South Africa. It would lead me to say yes to motherhood—nursing my babies, enriching their lives with trips to botanical gardens, hiking paths where the only prints were baboon or mongoose, the only sounds surf pounding. Ultimately it led me to Minnesota, the delight of paddle in hand, northern lights, loon songs, joy of sweaty body cradled by water. My original yes to love when I was first born again, echoed into other yeses.

⌒

I arrived in England on September 29, 1973. I was twenty-one years old. Someone had given me some English pounds from their aunt's husband. I had a plane ticket. My parents took me to the airport in Vancouver, and I waved goodbye and got on the plane.

My first letter home, dated Sept. 30, 1973:

After I got off the plane, I got a bus downtown and then took a cab to the train station.

What a cab ride! Little winding streets, old, old row buildings—I thought I'd try to make a little conversation with the driver so as we passed a rather big building I said, "What's that?" He looked at me like I was first class weirdo, and said, "That is Buckingham Palace." He then proceeded to give me a first-class commentary on all the famous places in London—Trafalgar Square, Big Ben, British Museum (huge). All in about 15 minutes' time. My eyes were bugging. Coming over, not especially to see the sites, I had almost forgotten they were there. I stepped onto the Nottingham train just as it pulled out.

In Nottingham, very dark outside, pouring down rain. Someone directed me to a bus station where I waited for a bus to Bramcote. At the station a girl who worked in a factory and her friend sat down next to me and asked me something. I answered, and she said (accusingly), "You're an American" and proceeded to tell me all about Americans. So, I went and stood and waited for the bus. I had had nothing to eat all day except a peppermint one of the spinsters on the train had given me. It was about eight, pouring rain and my arms were aching from the luggage. I began to think I'd gone bananas to come over. The bus driver said he'd drop me at St. John's but accidently drove by it, so he let me out on an extremely narrow dark road, with no sidewalk and said, "it's down that way."

So, I wandered along. Fortunately I had no alternative but to go on and found the college and knocked on a door—turned out to be the cook. She called the principal and he came up immediately and gave me a jolly English hug and kiss and we sat down for coffee. Then brought me over to the dorm, showed me around, put all the bedding on the bed. I said, "I'll do that." "You'll do nothing of the sort," said he.

I fell into a deep sleep. And woke this morning to a new world.

Waking that first morning stands as a key turning in my life. This time god had pulled me in over my head. I stir in my small cell to an eerie clanging. I pull back the curtain, swing the window open—a new world. Waves of homesickness dodge the strange sound. Bells.

Was it just the day before that I'd turned, weeping, and waving at my mother and father? The flight attendant checking my boarding pass must have thought I'd lost a loved one, when in fact I'd lost my life.

❦

I'd had no idea what to put into that suitcase. When I looked at the brochure "St. John's College, Nottingham" mimeographed onto buff paper, I couldn't tell who would be there, what it would be like to spend a year at a small Anglican seminary. But one treasure I zipped into an inside pocket—a cassette tape, blue ink scratched on—*Nine Lessons and Carols.* This was my visa, unlocking a new world.

Where was the god who had kicked me out of the nest of fundamentalism, of home, of small town western Washington, and plunked me down here?

I stand at that window, a black hole open to an alien landscape.

I drown in the gaping emptiness. Homesickness. As if someone had crept into my small cell in the night and gutted me, slipping out my vitals. "I cannot do this," I sob. "I cannot be here. Not for a year, not for a month, not for a day, not even for this hour."

All the reading I'd done (British novels for heaven's sake), the British movies I'd seen—they bore no relation to this landscape. Even the word "landscape" misses, skims; points to a shallow surface scraping, a stage set that could be taken down and pulled to another place.

Standing there, I thought I was aching for home, family, mountains. No, the truth was this: if the world framed here existed, I could never go home again. If god had called me to this . . . no, the bells were not calling the faithful to matins but tolling the death of my narrow, comfortable life. This god could only be trusted to pull me out of my depth—over and over.

The view this window ought to have framed—seagulls riding updrafts, distant vistas of Mt. Baker—this was already beginning to fade from my vision. I had lived my childhood years in a Western Washington scape/ scrape only a few inches deep. No before, no roots. The oldest building in Bellingham was the old tannery, dated 1894. My forebears had sprung up from North Dakota overnight and tumbled west.

What kind of god lived here, rather than in the wide spaces?

What this window framed was a world of ancient leaden bells, tolling, measuring life: sounds flung through the air, gonging death, ringing flood warning, pealing war's end. For hundreds of years, the crashing, melding, clashing overtones had soaked the countryside, twisted into the gnarled roots of great sycamores, rung in the ears of the dead. News buzzing on the earth's scape echoed deep, embracing ancient stones, and whispering to those in the grave.

I was used to skimming surfaces, schussing down slopes. But now I had entered a haunted place, and I felt it. My fingers would trace the mossy writing on gravestones, "Emily, mother 1712 . . ." Emily here, her body, her life, her death. Piled, cheek by jowl, countless rows in churchyards; I walked past them on my way to the White Lion Pub.

My new god had brought me to a place where I breathed the same air as people who had dreaded the rumored plague, cowered from Viking rampages, mourned sons lost in civil war; with those laced by Victorian respectability, suffocated by Great War mustard gas, crouched, hiding away from German bombing raids. These had all shared this space where my modern little cell now hung suspended in a four-story block. Their vapors were here: the child nursing in 1549; the worker laughing with his mates, 1912; the Celt, searching for firewood on a winter evening, 980. Layer upon layer upon layer.

My father's family, uprooted from Sweden, scraped the surface of the earth in North Dakota, exposed to sun, rain, snow, and wind. And then the dust. Living on the surface they failed to see how crucial those intertwining roots were, melding life's mat together. "Gosh darn it's hard to break up this land," they cursed the prairie. The native people knew what they didn't—that it was the woven roots that held. My poor disoriented forebears (thousands of miles from the cemeteries that held their beloveds' bones) dug for treasure and found dust. And rolled on west.

My faith had been as shallow as my father's crops—the surface of a reference Bible from which you could flip past hundreds of pages; stupid repetitive choruses, indicative of a history going back five years. How could I dive into this depth? Would god hold me?

Standing at that window on that Sunday morning, there was so much I didn't know, and didn't even know I didn't know: egg cups, ales, cathedrals, and private schools that were called public schools. About shopping at the greengrocers and the butchers and taking your own shopping bag and cycling with laden handlebars.

⌖

That morning at that window, a crack between worlds yawned, into which the warning vibrations and overtones of those bells vibrated my very core, warning me of the cost of the "yes" I was saying. I couldn't glimpse what might follow. The bells faded, and I turned, pulled on some clothes, and emerged into this new world. Be it unto me . . .

That evening I finished a perky letter home:

I had a good sleep, but boy are these rooms cold. 3 blankets, a coat, and my bathrobe. Michael "collected" me for breakfast this morning after a couple hours of homesickness. His wife and kids are very nice. I didn't know how to attack an egg in an egg cup so the whole group gave me a lesson. Then we went down to church in Bramcote village—lovely old church—[bells] change ringing and all in a charming English village. The campus is also lovely—never know you were near a city. I'm such an amateur at Anglican services so it was a little amusing. I met two fellows from Massachusetts—one a Harvard grad and they and Michael and I walked up from church together and then went to coffee with the guys in a common room, other people where there, concerned, nice, then we had a Bible study which was so good . . . lots of prayer and concern and I felt like I have close friends already. Then to lunch which was actually dinner—met some great people then for coffee at the flat of a few of the couples. Just now went to high tea which is supposed to be like supper, I guess—bread and jam, egg and tomato sandwiches and cake with tea.

The atmosphere is terribly friendly and concerned. I sometimes have trouble understanding people they talk so fast and use odd words. There are 7

Americans in college and four Canadians, also several from South Africa. The toilet paper is like wax paper. Not many single people here yet. Probably about 13 girls in all. Lots of children here this weekend.

England is quite different from America—the streets are very narrow, with instead of intersections, rounds with several roads branching off, "round-abouts," they're called.

No one here has ever head a name like Mary Ellen—every time I have to repeat it—oh two Christian names stuck together, eh?

I just opened my window to let the change ringing from the local church in—it's awfully nice to hear so close.

This morning I had my doubts, but I'm beginning to think I'll like it here. The people are so warm—I've drunk so much coffee and tea that I'm ready to float away—the Christian atmosphere is fantastic—just right for me—very committed to the Lord, but also very human and warm. Love, Mary Ellen

When I'd first told my parents about my idea of going to England to study, my mom had said, "I'm afraid you'll marry a vicar." "What's a vicar?" I'd asked.

9

God with a British Accent

THIS NEW GOD SPEAKS with a different accent. Going to the village church, the worship is worlds away from "His banner over me is love," and "Lord, we really just claim . . ." Instead the Vicar's reedy voice: "O Lord, open thou our lips," and women in twin sets and pearls, responding, "And our mouths shall shew forth thy praise." The vicar again: "O God make speed to save us." And the women bent in their old coats and pillbox hats intoning, "O Lord make haste to help us." Together, over the smell of old prayer books, *Hymns Ancient and Modern*, leather kneelers: "Glory be to the Father, and to the Son, and to the Holy Ghost. As it was in the beginning, is now and ever shall be. World without end. Amen." Is this the "heaping up of empty phrases" I'd been warned about?

Not only does this god talk funny; he is way more lenient. He doesn't mind people going to the pub or playing tennis just for fun. Good Christians drinking beer! And the divine in England has different priorities: poverty rather than the rapture? Apartheid rather than a six-day creation? And if this god is so dissimilar, what would be asked of me? Even the question disorients me.

I whirl through those first few weeks amazed and delighted by people's tiny homes, toilets with chilly toilet seats and waxy toilet paper, little shops with no shopping bags. I love the public foot paths through fields with ancient mounds, factories on the skyline, cows who amble up to me when I clamber over a stile. (Stile—who knew there were really stiles except in nursery rhymes?!)

I am dizzyingly confused. Instead of "Hi, how are you?" people say, "Are you all right?" I touch my face, wondering if I have blood dripping. After a few days I begin to see a pattern when people look at me shocked when I say, "Do you think it's okay if I wear pants to church?" or "Let me just go get some pants on . . ." Ah, "pants" in England means "undies." The word you're looking for is "trousers."

A second-year student takes me to the old bike shed and helps me find a rusty Raleigh left by a recent grad. As I disentangle the slightly bent one speed—I chuckle remembering my beautiful racing bike I'd sold to finance being here. Cycling is not a sport but a mode of transport: I concentrate to stay on the correct side of road and speed around the roundabouts with cars and trucks and bikes weaving in and out.

I take the bus into downtown Nottingham—the centre as they call it—and get off at Maid Marian Way, gawking at the Old Trip to Jerusalem Pub, hundreds of years old. I go into a tea shop and order crumpets, "Ah, ya mean pyclettes . . ."

Twelve young women live on the top floor of the seminary. The "girls" (as I would have called them then) are a strange group; many like me have a call to ministry years before women are ordained. There were two from South Africa—South Africa!—I try not show I don't know South Africa is a country. Two are reading theology with no clear idea why—they shock me with their off-color jokes. Three from Yorkshire amuse me by saying in their northern accents, "moody poodles."

Two glass milk pints are delivered to our kitchen common room for all of us to share. Proud I have figured out how to open one—thumb in foil on top—I pour some onto my cereal and look around at scandalized faces. This is my first encounter with milk that has cream on top and it is clearly a cardinal rule (taught at your mother's knee) that a person tip the bottle back and forth before opening it. It has never occurred to me that milk doesn't come out of a cow pasteurized, homogenized, and 2 percent.

Felicity invites me home for a half-term weekend in late October. Her parents own a pub and live above it near Oxford. We cycle into town for her graduation pictures and then her graduation. So exotic . . . parading around, putting furred hoods on people. The calendar on her parents' kitchen door is marked and reads, "Felicity home with AMERICAN!!"

I offer to babysit for some married students. Their instructions say I can give the kids orange squash. Puzzled, I ask the children and they show me where the bottle of neon orange concentrate is kept. I pour each of them a glass straight up. They gaze at me in wonder and awe. I find out later that I've joined a long-standing parent/child feud—parents diluting the concentrate for economy and health's sake, and kids wanting their squash sweeter and stronger. I am the best babysitter ever!

One person in my small group invites several of us to Sunday afternoon tea with his wife and two children. Walking the mile back to college, other students mutter, "Very nice for those who can . . ." "La de da . . ." "Pretty nifty, I'd say . . ." The detached house the couple has purchased for their seminary years is considered a profligate luxury. To my American eyes it appears nice but smallish.

Shopping, I try to figure out sizes which seem vast in centimeters. I look for shoes, asking for size ten, and people look at me and my feet in wonder telling me they have no women's shoes that big. Odd, I think, that a whole population's feet could be that much smaller, until around shop number four it occurs to me that the sizes are different.

Classes are exhilarating—parables, apologetics, Old Testament—smart people discussing crucial texts! St. John's Theological College is seen as very progressive since they have hired a tutor to teach pastoral care, a woman! We sit on cushions on Anne's floor and talk about how we *feel* about our lives and callings. The public school-educated guys squirm and share about the trauma of being shipped off to boarding school at an early age. We learn to respond to people, "Do I hear you saying you felt really upset?" "It seems to me you are saying you felt bereft."

One Sunday morning my pastoral care assignment is on the women's gynecology ward at the local hospital. I walk up to a bed and say (brightly), to the woman lying there: "How are you today?"

"Oh, love," she says. "I'm fine from the surgery, but it's this wind." I glance toward the windows and see trees outside, still, as if they'd been painted on the sky.

I smile knowingly, "Well, God bless."

And move a few beds along to ask another woman how she is doing. "It's the wind, dearie," she says. I look out again. This is supposed to be women's gynecology and I have ended up on a psychiatric ward. After a third attempt gets the same response, I spot one of my seminary colleagues and grab him. "Wind. Does 'wind' mean something other than . . ." I make a motion like tree branches. He bursts out laughing. "I think you call it gas."

Even with the question of "wind" cleared up, I was befuddled by the most common question women on that ward ask me: "Courting, ducks?" (Are you dating anyone, sweetie?)

We meet in small groups with a tutor for morning worship; other Anglican seminaries gather to recite Matins. Some complain we are not really being prepared for the church as it is, but I can't imagine rattling off more moldy old prayer book stuff, when you could be really sharing.

I continue to write perky letters home.

The weather was nice, so Marion and Felicity and I took a walk. There's a lovely trail near the college (called a public footpath) that goes between and through fields and over fences (stiles) and down through old golden trees and by a cemetery and an old, old church—very pretty. Taking walks like that with natives is odd, because the things I notice, they don't. One of the sights that amazes me is all the chimneys—miles and miles, all the same old fancy chimneys. Anyhow the path took us to another village, Stapleford, where we bought cheese and eggs and scones for supper. It started to rain so we caught a double decker bus part way back and then got soaked. Came into our common room and had tea while it poured and there was a big thunder and lightning storm. Then cooked supper.

An English custom, something like Thanksgiving, not a specific Sunday, at the local church called harvest is today. Chris a cockney girl who sounds like My Fair Lady, BEFORE mind you, and I are going to service and then to take around harvest time gift baskets to poor people.

I said I didn't know the queen was married because I hadn't heard of the king—that really killed them—they laughed for days.

We started talking about food—American food to them equals hot dogs, hamburgers, grits, and pancakes. One of the fellows is called Taffy—means welsh—and he said he'd heard there was a kind of candy you roasted over a fire—none of them had ever seen or roasted marshmallows.

Lunch and then field hockey! What fun! There are 7 guys and 2 girls on our team, nine guys on the Trent Polytechnic team we played. They beat us 7-2. From what the guys said, the other team was little unethical in its treatment of us ladies and very rough. I really loved it though. You have to charge at the team as they come at you to try to get the ball.

At one point I got a nasty crack on the forehead by running head on into a bloke—really knocked me flat. Dave, one of the guys from St. John's with a real cockney accent, started in, "Ya all right Mary Ellen; hey fellas, who's going to give a kiss to revive the lady? Line up here—come on blokes!" at which point I jumped up. We have a match almost every Wednesday from now on.

People here are very different about money. They are very concerned about rising materialism and are careful not to get into it, like Christians in the states are careful not to get drunk. The professors have small houses, old cars, and black and white TV. People here, many of them, have given up high paying jobs to go into the ministry, which isn't high paying at all—1200 pounds a year is the norm, I think.

There is real concern especially about working-class materialism.

There is a wider division between classes—at first, I thought that it was mostly in the way they were looked at; I think, though, from talking to people that the working class is largely separate, and mostly of a whole different way of thinking.

Oh well, who knows? Maybe a rich and handsome young vicar will have swept me off my feet. (Tee-hee-hee-hee.) But don't hold your breath.

Love, Mary Ellen

10

Your God Is Too Big

THIS NEW GOD HAS turned my world upside down: I am dizzied by different landscapes, manners, concerns, language.

I'm fearful—are these people "Bible-believing"? My old idol was contained within the pages of the "wordagod." Do these Brits know Jesus is the only way? The god I am meeting here shoulders responsibility not only for me (and members of the fellowship), but for people from Africa and Asia.

And I'm rubbing shoulders with people whose life experience could hardly be more different from mine—guys who went to Eton, others who grew up without plumbing.

I can't begin to grasp a god who is so much bigger, if I'm to believe what I'm learning in classes and life. This god goes back way further than the 6,000 years I'd learned in my fundamentalist Bible studies, and is way less clear on the end times.

I have no idea how to grow into this gigantic god.

Tiny, constricted country England is, but it had put me onto a broad plain where anything could happen. As I met people from all over the world, I began to see that this god could send me anywhere, call me to anything. Six months before I hadn't been able to fathom why anyone would ever leave Western Washington—mountains, Puget sound—what more did you want? Here I was in a whole new world. My profound disorientation—dizzied by different worship, theology, lifestyle, language, history, people—all of this had me casting around for firm ground.

And god answered, by miraculously bringing a man into my life who could guide and stabilize me.

‿ତ

By the time my parents got that letter jokingly mentioning a vicar who might sweep me off my feet, god had brought the perfect man into my life. We were in the same apologetics class, and he seemed so intellectual when he spoke in class we all turned to look at him. People whispered that he had a PhD in the sciences. After class one day we went to lunch together and talked about our conversions—I told him my story and he told me about going to a Billy Graham crusade in Manchester, "to make fun of it," he said. And then god touched him. Here was someone who was so smart but also had a vital, living faith—bridging that divide that had nearly pulled me asunder.

E was brilliant, remembering almost everything he read, arguing so logically that people were awed by his mind. We sat in The White Lion and I asked him about evolution, which I'd been taught was the work of the devil since the Bible says god created the world in six days. He patiently explained (over his pint of bitter and my beer shandy) about how god can use many methods do his work, and that the Bible is not meant to be a scientific document and how we read different texts in different ways. The sheer stimulation of this discussion, putting to rest my fear of believing, felt to me like skiing North Face at Mt. Shuksan on a beautiful day.

Despite his shrunken leg from polio, E liked to play tennis and bike and hike. We cycled to a local site—Wollaston Manor—and walked around, admiring the views. On Saturdays we went with friends who had a car to the Peak District and walked five or six miles, ending up at a pub for supper.

Our differences seemed romantic, intriguing. For him, I was completely outside the rigid norms of England; for me he represented this new world I'd fallen in love with.

I could not even begin to peer into that deepest chasm of all in England—class. Strange how our Christian faith—based on the earliest church's baptismal formula: "In Christ there is no longer Jew nor Gentile, slave nor free, male nor female,"[1]—the vastest bifurcations of first-century society, couldn't begin to touch this. Here in England and throughout the empire, class was supreme, an apartheid so pervasive it was almost invisible.

Different manners—how you put your milk in your tea; whether or not you sprinkled salt on your food or put a tiny pile of salt and pepper

1. Galatians 3:28.

on the side of your plate. These were sacramental—outward, visible signs of deep divides, indicators of your place in society and the world.

Class: Even in those first days, I could see some of my fellow students had a certain gift of the gab, flashes of sophisticated humor, a way of wearing a scarf flipped up and over. These young men had been raised to rule and civilize a benighted world, yet to know home to be England's green and pleasant land. Hundreds of years of Shakespeare and *The Book of Common Prayer* had flowed over them, day by day, a rhythm woven through British plays and novels, echoing in their privileged syntax.

And then those three or four whose accents were thicker and harder to understand, who stood on the edges, hollered their jokes, chewed with their mouths open, wore the wrong clothes. E was one of them. You could be clever, but you could never get it right, never hold the magic. Not in England; not even in the far-flung reaches of an empire where someone might recognize your low beginnings. Only in America were all British accents privileged and cute.

Classes were tumbled together in death, their vapors mingling, but during life, the chasm gaped. "How can you be so snobby?" I objected, the third or fourth time I heard someone in my small group say, "working class." My Oxbridge educated tutor called me into his office, where he sat deep in his leather chair surrounded by books and spoke of the cultural divide—how few working-class people attended church, read books, owned property. "Are you saying they are stuck there?" I demanded.

Manners, accents, dress, humor would always give them away, Julian said. I realized decades later he was warning me about my budding relationship with E, telling me news I refused to believe—that this fault line could prove dangerous. The Anglican Church was riddled with class guilt; successful churchmen did their obligatory couple years in a "rough area" to become eligible for a bishopric.

I visited E's hometown that New Year's Eve. I had never been to a working-class town, though E had told me how fifty years before, rain burned holes in sheets left out to dry, because of St. Helens' chemical factories. About long childhood evenings when his father took him to his sister's grave and then left him shivering on the pub steps.

Still I was knocked sideways by sheer ugliness: creeping lines of houses, miserable paved yards, smoke stacks. Clouds like blackout curtains trapped foul-tasting air. The "two up, two down" his parents had rented for forty years seemed bizarre—the coal fire, velvet painting of a Samoan woman, display cabinet with his mother's prize collection of plastic dolls in garish folk costumes. We faced the blaring telly, his parents smoking, his dad running to the chippy for mushy peas and fries, drinking endless cups of strong tea. I barely understood them: "Eeee, yerall roit Meery," they reassured me.

Finally, as the tea had its way, we left, since his parents were ashamed to have "the American" use their outdoor privy. Off to the mall, with its gaudy shops and pasty white children slouched in strollers. I pictured my love, a little boy with a mop of curls, sickly lungs, hobbling with his crutch across cobbled streets, under belching smoke stacks.

My revulsion for St. Helens fueled my admiration: how heroic to escape the dearth of academic, religious, aesthetic sense! His cleverness had been rewarded. In those days a small proportion of students tested at certain ages were streamed toward higher, all-expense-paid education and E had tested into grammar school, A levels, University, a PhD, and then called to ordination. What a story! From the grimness of St. Helens, I would take this poor limping boy, with no social skills (how could he—look at his family!) to realms where he could breathe deep and be loved into life.

His background, his wounds didn't matter, since, like me, he was a new person in Christ! His polio at age two (months in an isolation ward with no touch), reconstructive surgeries in Liverpool where his car-less parents struggled to visit, years of being laughed at for his crippled leg, his mother's detachment, his father's alcoholism—these were nothing. Even the inferiority complex of a working-class boy in a middle-class world (university, seminary)—these would be healed!

I believed my love could heal his stunted heart. Brilliant, he could have changed the landscape of genetics but had nobly chosen to follow god's call. And this same god had chosen me to be his helpmeet! What could possibly go wrong?

11

Needing a Fairy-Tale God

WE WISH FOR A magical god, who guarantees health and happiness, sorts out errant spouses and children, and reveals a clear future. When circumstances—disease, divorce, or death—introduce new/contradictory information, there are a few options. We might stretch the overall story by finding a redeeming circumstance—someone who accepts Jesus after seeing you handle your daughter's demise, for example. We might assume that things will be sorted out in the hereafter, with more stars in your crown. The story stretches.

My new god had delivered me to this new world, but I still functioned as a fundamentalist. Momentous choices—going to England, marrying—I had little to do with them, except to walk through doors opened by god. In fact, my passivity demonstrated my trust in god, since side-stepping responsibility was an act of faith.

Going to England? I HAPPENED to listen to nine lessons and carols at a crisis point in my faith; and then MIRACULOUSLY find a brochure for Regent College in my car. And ended up IN LINE next to the seminary principal; my great aunt COINCIDENTALLY offered me money. Against all odds, God had brought me to St. Johns, Nottingham, pretty much plunked me down there, so when I met E, it all made sense.

Placid passivity on the surface, but just beneath bubbled my intense creativity, anger, passion, and idealism. The sweet child who had burned with zeal—to end world hunger, to rescue someone from impending death—stilled lived within.

But I knew that, as a woman, I had been designed by god to support a man's calling, to charm, to bake. Since it was against the will of God for a woman to be in ministry, any tugs I felt in that direction were clearly suspect. Instead I would be a vicar's wife! The miraculous clarity of E's call provided ample shirt-tails for me to ride on.

⌒

E and I visited some parishes needing curates—Leatherhead, Oxford, Leeds—but E assured me that since God hadn't given him a sense of clarity about going there, they weren't right for us. I loved having someone who could make decisions for me.

Our best friends were Graham and Gill—Graham was at St. John's with us but had been born in South Africa. Gill was from a posh London suburb and they were planning their June wedding. We spent a week on Skye with them, and although their wedding was very formal—with a footman who announced guests!—they helped E and I plan ours.

I wrote to my mom—could you get someone to do the flowers? Could you find someone to make a cake? I wrote to Pete—could you sing "To God be the Glory"? The idea of premarital counseling was ridiculous, of course, since God had brought us together. What about a cake? Flowers? Liturgy? We hiked through the countryside and cooked haggis in the evening. Back to college, we frantically wrote papers, had the equivalent of a graduation, and flew to America.

My marriage was a way to sign on with a god who had everything under control.

E met my parents for the first time. A Brit! With a PhD! One who was going to be a vicar!

We used the newly reworked *Anglican Service for Holy Matrimony.* A neighbor did the flowers with a circlet of roses for my hair to match my homemade wedding dress—full length with long sleeves, ruffles, and tiny pink roses on a white background. College friends Flo and Mary Lou wore long pink jumpers with white blouses underneath. E's seminary friend Pete flew in from England. Ladies from the church put on the reception with coffee, green sherbet punch, pastel mints, cake, and nuts.

After we changed—my going away outfit was a blouse I'd bought at Penney's and some old jeans—we drove forty-five minutes to catch the last ferry to Orcas Island where I'd arranged a cottage for our honeymoon. "This is your honeymoon?" the resort owner asked. "Here's some home-made ginger beer."

I slipped out of bed early that first morning of my married life and walked the rocky shore. The tide was out, so I looked at anemones, starfish, sea cucumbers while E slept. We hadn't thought to bring books—do you read on a honeymoon? After two days we were bored and decided to head back to the mainland and our new apartment. E caught a salmon with my dad's help; we hiked up Church Mountain switchback after switchback. E began working for Smith's Gardens, hauling, weeding, lifting, and became very tan and fit. I went back to my job at the Whatcom County Library.

We went back to my old church—First Presbyterian—where people loved E's accent. When he preached, people hung on his every word, and I blushed when he said things like, "I don't know if you have marbles here— they are small glass spheres," not noticing people's bemused expressions. I chuckled along with them.

An exotic blue aerogram arrived in September, from Bruce Evans, rector of a large parish in Cape Town, saying someone had suggested E for a job there. In seminary there had been several South Africans and we knew something of the struggle: E nodded knowingly, "If I went there I'd be arrested!" We read the letter and put it away.

Surely this God, who had brought us together against all odds had a plan for us! Daily we prayed, "God please guide us." We went to our jobs, lived in our tiny apartment. I tried recipes like Singapore Satay, Double Chocolate Pound Cake, Sweet and Sour Pork. How could I feel lonely and restless, when I had married the man God had chosen for me?

Constant Pacific Northwest drizzle: clouds pulled down like blinds. We worked at our jobs and it seemed like maybe god had forgotten us. Paul had written, "Be anxious for nothing," and I claimed that verse, but it didn't seem to work. My old childhood terrors resurfaced. Shouldn't being married to this rational, brilliant man, not to mention my year of theological study, have cured me of anxiety? When I told my mom I was struggling she told me now that I was a wife I needed to pull myself together.

In December E told me that we couldn't be praying "God guide us" without being willing to go to South Africa. He wrote a cautious letter to Cape Town and dropped it in the mail. We waited for a response. As soon as we dropped the letter in the mail, saying we were willing to pray about going, god gave us enthusiasm about it. Or at least that was the story we told afterwards to show how clear it was that god wanted us in Cape Town. Gray days rolled by, and we pulled our enormous '62 Chevy up to the line of mail boxes at the Hawaiian Village. I opened the box, knowing there would be a blue aerogram in it, but nothing.

By March we were desperate. We'd heard nothing from Cape Town, so we decided to go job hunting in England. We looked for jobs for E—each one seemed promising but proved fatally flawed—the church in Edinburgh needed someone who could chant the service or the church in Oxford needed someone who could work with youth. We left England thinking there might be a job in Durham and returned to Bellingham to find the funding for the position had been withdrawn. I felt completely abandoned by god, but E explained to me that this could not possibly be the case. We were being tested.

In June we heard from Cape Town and knew this was the call of god. Of course, god hadn't failed us!

PART THREE

12

At Sea with God

1995: STEVE LOOKS AT pictures curling in an album.

Mom, how old were you when you moved to South Africa?

Twenty-three.

Are you kidding?

No. I'm not kidding. Just after our first anniversary—that would have been 1975—we left Bellingham, Washington, flew to England, and boarded the *Pendennis Castle*. We had been offered a job in South Africa's Anglican Church.

I know what you're thinking, Steve. Fortunately, I knew a lot. I knew that South Africa was on the southern tip of Africa. I'd read *Cry the Beloved Country* and *Too Late the Phalarope* by Alan Paton. And a brochure—"The History of South Africa"—written by the South African government's propaganda department, explaining how white Afrikaners had arrived minutes before native tribes swept down from farther north in Africa. So they got there first.

Not to mention the really important knowledge: I'd spent three years studying the "wordagod" almost every evening as a fundamentalist, a year at an Anglican seminary in England, and a year being a wife.

I was twenty-three, but unusually wise and mature. (Not "the wisdom of the world," of course. God's wisdom, remember, was wiser than the wisdom of man.) Now that we were clear about our call, everything would be fine.

Your Dad and I, Steve, would live happily ever after, since we were both deeply committed Christians. I knew about marriage. I had read several books on the subject. *Christian* books on *Christian* marriage. I knew how to be a good wife. Any cultural differences between us (since he was British, I American, he working class, I middle class) were nothing, since we were both new creatures in Christ. Our problematic childhoods—behold, those had passed away as we had become new!

What made it easy to move from western Washington State to South Africa was the fact that this was God's plan. God had brought us together—that was clear—dropping me at an Anglican seminary in Nottingham, England. What were the chances?

That evening in October, 1973: sitting next to each other, watching *Elvira Madigan* at the local arts theater, I knew he was the one. The next night we danced till midnight at a college party. The day after we prayed about our relationship. It was incredible how we—from such different backgrounds—agreed about everything! We were soulmates! How wonderfully our hormones pointed to the will of God!

God had called me to marry E and to become his 'helpmeet'—that good old King James Version label for helper or aid, like God had given Adam. We were meant for each other.

Yes, god had brought the perfect man into my life and I knew it. He was so smart—he had a PhD, for heaven's sake. He was ultra-rational. Three days after our first date, I told him I was feeling down. "May I ask you a somewhat personal question? Where are you in your menstrual cycle?" My emotional ups and downs, my vibrant imagination, all could be held in check by this man!

It was perfect! For years I had snuck into the pulpit of the First Presbyterian Church to preach passionately to an empty church. But these impulses were unladylike and wrong. "I permit not a woman to teach," Paul had written.[1] God had given us a chain of command, to guide, shape, and protect us. A woman must always be under a man's authority; until she married, she was under her father's authority. (If that parent thoughtlessly died, leaving her unprotected, she would need to ask her pastor to play this role.)

Even though I'd turned away from fundamentalism and gone to an Anglican seminary, I could not have been called to ministry because the church did not ordain women. But I could be a vicar's wife! An outstanding vicar's wife!

All we had to do was to trust god. And now god had called us to go to South Africa.

---

1. 1 Timothy 2:12.

We were ready. Ready to go to South Africa under apartheid. To a country where I would find the standing joke true: "You are now arriving in South Africa; please set your watches back thirty years." Ready to take my marriage from the Hawaiian Village Apartments in Bellingham, (where I'd only once met a black person). Ready to leave my job at the Whatcom County Library and move to Cape Town where my visa meant I couldn't work. Ready to go from First Presbyterian Church in Bellingham to St. John's Parish, Wynberg—a large, multiracial parish grappling with religion, politics, and looming revolution. Ready to begin having a family.

I packed a box of wedding gifts—a flan dish, a candle snuffer, salt and pepper shakers, some floral sheets. My most dramatic problem arose when the postal worker in Bellingham made me completely unpack my box because of size restrictions. People behind me in line watched, shuffling. I fumed at her. Couldn't she see we were called?

The stories we tell ourselves orient us within our world. My fairy-tale belief as I sailed to South Africa—if I'm good, god will not let anything bad happen to me—might be false, but it was comforting and gave me an illusion of control. The fairy-tale made embarkation possible, literally and metaphorically.

We'd been called, and the god who calls us would look after us. It was that simple. I told my mom not to worry.

⟶⟵

We flew to England and took a train to St. Helens. England seemed cramped and smelly after the Pacific Northwest.

We bought a large trunk from what was once St. Helen's company store. Waiting to pay for it, E told me how he and his mother had queued for two hours to buy silk stockings after the war, only to have them run out just as they got to the front of the line.

We packed the trunk with some clothes and books we'd stored in the attic of E's parents' tiny "two up, two down." We've been told to divide our luggage in two groups—"not wanted on voyage," which would go into the hold, and what we'd need for the ten days on board. E's brother borrowed a van and drove us to Southampton.

Our tickets, sent by the church in Cape Town read: "Depart Southampton, Friday 5 September. Thursday 18 Sept. arrive Cape Town."

The *Pendennis Castle* was one of the "mail ships" that for years delivered goods and people to the colonies, stopping only at Tenerife in the Canary Islands, because as a South African ship it must sail outside coastal waters. As we climb on board and find our cabin, it doesn't occur to me that this ship goes to a country that is over 90 percent black, yet there is not one person of color—passengers or crew—on the *Pendennis Castle*.

Most passengers are rich holiday-makers going out by ship and flying back to England some months later. Some are young couples emigrating from England in hopes of sunshine, a swimming pool, and domestic help. Some, like us, are going out to do god's work.

There is a first-class section in the bow, and early in the morning dividers are opened so people can walk laps around the deck: I feel like I'm watching an old black and white movie about a young couple on a boat to another country with a whole cast of strange people. I'm in a time capsule, playing a part in an historical reenactment, with Divine Service led by Captain Cattersall in the First-Class Lounge. He stands tall in his uniform and rattles off the service, straight out of the old prayer book—"very much the proper thing to do." He could also do burials at sea if necessary. I'm at sea—literally and metaphorically—but when people ask us where we're going we show none of that. Because we've been so clearly called by god, our only response can be "Aye, aye, sir."

I look at a menu sheet: Breakfast has a few fruit and cereal options, but then "Smoked Finnan Haddock Poached in Milk," eggs done in a number of ways, bacon, "country black pudding," creamed potatoes, fried bread, fresh toast, ham, sausage, jam, marmalade . . .

Dinner has several options for starters, including consommé, followed by the fish course, then pasta, veal, chicken, sirloin, potatoes, beans, plus a cold buffet and salads and sweets like trifle followed by a savory "Croute Windsor" or "Croute Diane." We ask our server about these and he shrugs, "Cheese on toast." Or he shakes his head when we ask about a menu item, "I wouldn't touch it if I were you." or "Won't you see you at breakfast if you eat that." Carafes of red or white wine are sixty pence.

Our assigned tables for the second seating are next to an English bobby and his wife and two children. They are very jolly about sunshine and a swimming pool. Has he thought about the transition from being an English bobby to a member of the South African police force who are trained to shoot protesters?

Besides walking on the deck early in the morning and eating, there are entertainments. "Programme of Main Events: Southampton to Cape Town" Voyage no. 119 Tourist Class. There are professional dancers on board with "Dancing to Modern Records." There's a beauty shop and cinema every few nights with some sort of movie.

I write to my parents:

The evenings are really lovely on board—it's so warm that late at night you can stand on deck in a quite heavy wind with just a dress and feel toasty warm. The sun seems very penetrating.

After breakfast we had a real answer to prayer about meeting some Christians—on the notice board was a sign about a non-denominational, short devotional meeting each day 11:00–11:45. So we went and met so many nice Christians. In a situation like this, the difference is really quite striking—so many of the non-Christians are mostly interested in booze, gambling, etc.

Afterward up on deck we met some more—a really nice young couple that've just finished Bible College in England.

These were the ones who two years later were shot in Rhodesia.

We watch flying fish and see fishing boats from Sierra Leone. There's a party to celebrate crossing the equator: I've never known anyone who's crossed the equator. Hot and humid with no air conditioning in tourist class, we slide a big piece of cardboard into our porthole to get some breeze into our cabin. We're told that the derivation of the word *posh* comes from these ships—people knowing to get their cabins "port out, starboard home" to catch the breezes. We become friends with the man who is going to be the Anglican chaplain to the tiny island of Tristan da Cunha. I write to my parents: *"Deck quoits (kind of like shuffleboard) is good . . . choosing names for a dog when we get to Cape Town. We're going to inquire about the regulations for bringing them back in to the U.S."* Definitely planning to stay briefly . . .

I am so out of my depth . . . and then the Cape rollers, as the waves rocking the ship from behind are fondly called, hit us, and I take to my bed for a few days.

No sight of land for ten days and then we arrive in Cape Town during the night. In the morning I look out the porthole at Table Mountain—the mystery, inspiration, and compass point for my next seven years.

13

Where Is God in the Midst of Evil?

WHEN LIFE GROWS MORE complicated, the temptation to simplify grows too. The truest stories are convoluted, streaked with mixed motives, unresolved childhood experiences, parental messages, societal norms—confounding the "simple story."

Fear makes people conservative: faced with extreme stress, people often clamp down their belief system. Moving to a country halfway around the world during a time of looming revolution, it was all I could do to hold onto my god.

The story I told myself during those early years in South Africa was as simple as I could make it. Looking at photos unearthed from this time, my daughter-in-law says, "Mary Ellen, you look so serious, so unhappy, compared to the Mary Ellen I know now." The sheer exhaustion of disorientation, the lack of the firm footing of work, and my loneliness within the constant stream of people streaming through the house. But I could never have said I was unhappy since that might have implied I wasn't trusting god's call to this country, to my vocation as vicar's wife, to my marriage.

Framed by the porthole, Table Mountain at dawn looms secretive and bulky. I was twenty-three and would look up to her daily until I was thirty. She was an Eden—untouched by the human greed and fear bubbling around her base.

We walk down the gangway and are met by people from the church, who drive us from Cape Town Harbor, skirting the mountain, to the southern suburbs where we will live. As we drive I feel as if I'm watching a portentous travelogue of my life ahead.

We drive through central Cape Town's mix of flower sellers and old buildings, heading toward the suburbs sprawled around the part of Table Mountain called Devil's Peak. Turn the other way, our driver says, and you would get to Sea Point on the chilly Atlantic Ocean. Mostly Jews and Afrikaners live there. Head in this direction, he tells us, you find mainly English people, nearer to the warmer (but shark-infested) Indian Ocean beaches.

I would learn that these language/lineage divides were deeper than oceans, an apartheid within apartheid. My fellow English speakers were quick to inform me that the Afrikaners had designed apartheid—literally "separate development"—and were destroying this beautiful country. Those Afrikaners had developed the theology of apartheid to justify their evil treatment of blacks by saying it was god's design to uphold the purity of the race. The Afrikaners had a yearly celebration called the Day of the Covenant, which was the holiest of holy days to them: the remembrance of their covenant with god confirmed with the blood of thousands of Zulu warriors.

We drive through District Six, near Devil's Peak, which had been a thriving "coloured" neighborhood; its people had been cleared out by the Group Areas Act, but whites (who must have been English) refused to move there, so it had become an empty monument to the stupidity of apartheid.

This same Group Areas Act, I would learn, had cut lines around the mountain. In the first ring suburbs—*blanke* (white), of course—nestle huge architect-designed houses with spreading lawns, swimming pools, tennis courts, and servants' quarters, behind high walls, owned by English speaking whites.

The next circle—*blanke* too—is for those with white skin, but theirs is still tainted with the grey of their escape from Liverpool or Wigan or some other English working-class town.

A little further out—*nie blankes nie* (nonwhites only)—are areas for "coloured" folk who were a mixture of the Malay, Indian, white and black— who coexisted in the Cape for hundreds of years. Many of them have been cleared out of "white" areas, now occupied by immigrants from England.

Farther out on the sandy Cape flats are townships for the few Xhosa or Zulu allowed to live in Cape Town—Guguletu, Nyanga, and the squatter camps like Crossroads and later Kylitcha, with tin pieced together to shelter families. In the distance is Robben Island, where Nelson Mandela lives. I'm told it is dangerous to even mention his name.

The racial mixture of Cape Town could have been like the beauty of a gorgeous bouquet of protea, mixed with heather and freesia. But apartheid literally means separate, and how could you decide where someone could live if you didn't know exactly what race they were? Everyone was classified: my three children's birth certificates all read "white." Within this code of purity, miscegenation muddied the waters—sex across racial lines was illegal. And to keep people apart, beaches, trains, buses, shops, and benches were separate. Even churches had been told to segregate, but the Anglican Church had refused.

And the mountain went on being the mountain while the people went on being the people.

As we drove on, our driver pointed out the Rhodes memorial on the mountainside, with its classical pillars and statue of Rhodes mounted on his steed. Rhodes had explored, mined, and colonized Southern Africa from 1853 to 1903. Visiting later, I ponder that bronze man on his horse—frozen, it seems, just as he was heading north to continue his rape of southern Africa. His statue eyes look to the mountains beyond Stellenbosch and then the Karoo and the Kimberly diamond mines. He couldn't begin to see the gold mines of Johannesburg, or Pretoria, the seat of apartheid, nor beyond to his namesake country, Rhodesia (later Zimbabwe), and the rest of "black Africa." We were told stories of what happened to white people in those countries and so we kept our passports handy.

We drive that first day through Kenilworth, which would be our village—a quaint town from *Country Life* dropped into Southern sunshine. Over years, I would shop there, in Teales, which carried frightfully British women's sweaters and twin sets, along with coveralls for maids. Another shop sold imported fabrics, decorating items, and accessories from England. There is a butcher and a green grocer. When we had to really shop we went to Claremont to an American-style shopping centre or to the big Pick and Pay supermarket (pronounced "puk und pai").

Where was god in apartheid South Africa? A few hours after we disembark, I sit in the Rayner's lounge nursing my sixth cup of tea. Paul is priest in charge at St. Luke's, so this is his rectory. The blur of the boat, the arrival in the harbor, the drive through such different neighborhoods—bustling city, empty District 6, leafy suburbs, now a "coloured" area. Though I'm finally off the ship, I'm still dizzied and out of my depth.

I go into the bathroom and lock the door. I try to remember we have been called here. Okay, that's right. God has called—just when the letter dropped in the box we felt enthusiasm. And god is at work here. We'd heard stories, while we were still in seminary in Nottingham, about the dramatic movement of the spirit in South Africa, how many of the bishops had been touched by god—out of the blue. All these clergy and churches that had been Anglo catholic, social gospel, had now experienced the savior and wanted to immerse themselves in the Bible. No wonder god had called us!

⟷

I take a few deep breaths and go back into the living room crowded with white and coloured people. Because of their accents, I understand one word in five, but I'm very aware of my role as minister's wife, so I take another cup of tea and smile. Everyone wants to talk to me, because as an American I am still the stuff of movies.

When parishioners from St. Luke's leave, Margaret hands me my eighth cup of tea. She and Paul explain apartheid to us. Not only do I learn how it works but that it is not our fault. At all. It makes so much sense. Those bad Afrikaners. And if you get far enough away from them—like we are here in Cape Town—this paradise of mountains and sea is an Eden of races smiling at each other on train platforms! So many pleasant greetings. Now I understand. Completely.

That was the last time the tangle of culture, race, history, colonialism, and religion seemed clear and really, quite interesting. Before they become bewildering, pressing, even terrifying.

14

My God Is a Household God

PRIMITIVE PEOPLE CARRIED THEIR household gods when they moved. I traveled to south Africa clutching my intensely personal (and magical, please, please, please) god. My placating rituals shifted to a scone-making and tea-serving ceremony required to be an excellent vicar's wife.

My fundamentalist god left political involvement to the institutional church since Jesus was coming back any minute to get us out of this mess. Even St. John's parish (our particular parish within the Church of the Province of South Africa) had limited its political involvement, harboring a belief that god was more concerned with souls, though this was changing by the time we got there. But in those early days, this god—who called for systemic societal change or who appeared through the cracks in people's lives—might be too demanding and unreliable. He might forget that his prime responsibility was to keep me safe.

I see this in my letters, written (nearly) weekly to recount my experiences, since phone calls were so expensive they were reserved for Christmas or a baby's birth. Posting letters felt like throwing bottled messages into the ocean (Atlantic or Indian?). A castaway in South Africa, I was cut off in a way unimaginable in a world of email, Twitter, and Skype.

The Anglican Church disobeyed segregation orders, supported banned clergy, defied government conscription orders, and wrestled with Christianity's role in colonialism. I thought this was probably good, but I hoped these would not distract my god from his primary focus: me and my babies. After all, even in a world so full of hatred, fear, and impending blood bath, people still got cancer, babies were born, expenses piled up. It wasn't as if I didn't care: I simply could not stretch my arms around a god this big-hearted in my homesick and culture-shocked state.

Thirty years later—after immersion in colonial, feminist, literary and theological studies—the person writing these letters seems impossibly naïve. But she had to be. Many exclamation points helped convince her parents (and herself) god was keeping her safe. And they hid fear and guilt about inevitable complicity.

South Africa made less and less sense as the years went by. It grew increasingly difficult, and finally impossible, to keep my incorrigible household god inside, looking after only me.

Aerogram—September 19, 1975

The rectory has gorgeous gardens. Looking out the living room windows through a cascade of brilliant pink bougainvillea, I can just make out the pale blue of Table Mountain. There are five bedrooms, and maid's quarters—a maid lives there and wants to work, but I just don't know about it—seems kind of weird. Right behind our house is the church.

I awaken that first morning to two geckos moving gracefully across the ceiling.

Later that day, I stand in the kitchen, stocked to welcome us with packets of Bird's custard, tins of digestive biscuits, cans of peaches and beans, jars of marmite, loaves of bread. The fridge has milk, boervoers, cheese, eggs, and butter. Besides this enormous kitchen, there's a separate smaller kitchen—the scullery.

There is a tap on back door and a young woman shuffles in, her head lowered, wearing an orange and white plaid apron that buttons down the front. She mumbles something. "Good morning madam, good morning madam," I think. She has something—a nylon stocking pulled tight?—over her kinky hair. I reach out to shake her hand: "Hi, I'm Mary Ellen." She looks at me. "Madam." She touches her chest. "Caroline."

"No," I say. "Call me Mary Ellen. Please."

"Madam. When can I start working?" She tries a coy smile: with her two top front teeth removed, she looks like a child, though I later learn this is a sign of beauty within the "coloured" community.

"Caroline," I say. "You are welcome to live here and use the kitchen . . . but I can do the housework . . . I'm American and we do these things ourselves. But it's really nice to meet you."

She looks at me, shakes her head, and backs toward the door.

I've made a stand for egalitarianism, for American values. I'm no better than she is simply because my skin is white! How could I have someone cleaning my floors, just because they happened to be born in the wrong place at the wrong time?

The front doorbell rings and a beggar stands there. The Bible verse, "Give to everyone who asketh of you, give, expecting nothing in return" (Luke 6:30), rings in my head. But we've been warned not to give money, told that the rumors about a new family in the rectory would have spread far and wide, like painting a sign on the door: "Gullible Bleeding-Heart Newcomer."

I look at this man. He has an odd smell—unwashed? Alcohol? And yet I'm a Christian and Jesus calls us to care for the "least of these." Jesus loves him, I tell myself. He speaks, but I can't even tell if he's speaking English. He pulls up his shirt to show me a scar. Tears well up in his eyes and mine. Wait, I'll get you some food. I close the door. Should I have asked him to come in? What would Jesus do? The man sits on the step, eating his eggs and bacon and toast. He hobbles away on his crutches, and then tucks them under his arm and springs across a highway divider, waving to his friends.

I breathe deeply before I go out those first few days, driving on the wrong side, and I don't know my way around. I don't even realize that part of my disorientation is being in the southern hemisphere, where the sun shines from the north rather than the south. Fortunately, Table Mountain stands as a compass.

I can do this. I slip the car into reverse and then turn around and out onto Waterloo Road. Cars zip past but that's okay as I shift gears. I take the most direct route to a shop and park. I lock the car, go inside, and wander through the aisles, smelling strange smells and seeing packets with mysterious labels and pictures.

I stand in the aisle of the Pick and Pay, Wynberg, looking at flour. Before I can put anything in my cart, I have to try to figure out exactly what it is: American cornstarch is corn flour in England and maizena in South Africa. And how much does this cost in rands? Which would be how much in dollars? And grams, 750 grams is about how much in pounds? At the till I open my mouth and the cashier says, "American." That is (and will be) who I am to everyone I meet. "I had a cousin who went to America once. For two weeks." she confides. "How long have you been here?" "Two weeks," I say. "I love it."

The beauty of this physical landscape—steep mountainsides plummeting into ocean—delights me. So do church services—familiar *Book of Common Prayer* language and hymns—in accents that are less plummy, more nasally, than in England. People in the pews around me are darker than anyone I've ever worshiped with; and their accents! I'm told that you can tell someone's racial classification—(thank you, evil Afrikaners!)—more by accent than skin color.

How wonderful this Eden where people worship together across racial barriers even though it's illegal. Our parish is called St. John's Wynberg, with five churches. Three—St. John's, St. Luke's, and St. Phillips—are racially mixed: they are old churches and most of their members lived near them before the Group Areas Act. One—Emmanuel—is entirely "coloured" and one—Christ Church—is entirely "white." But all the churches gather regularly for worship and service projects. E has been called to be the assistant at Christ Church.

Church services are full: heartfelt, our voices braid us into a cause bigger than I've ever known. Deeply stirred, here am I Lord.

I ask a coloured couple after church an innocuous question: where do you live? They used to live near the church, they tell me. But they were forced to move out onto the sandy flats in the Group Areas Act. I widen my eyes in outrage. This would never happen in America.

The people I worshiped with that evening had been driven from their homes. For them, there was no escape from almost certain revolution. Waves of white doctors, professors, architects emigrated to New Zealand, Australia, Canada, and England. Many white South Africans I knew best (whose great, great grandparents had settled there) courageously chose to stay. But they were (like I was) benefitting—from the system. I gave thanks that I was from the land of the free and the home of the brave.

Before E's ordination, we visit some parishioners, to see firsthand the challenges faced by the church.

We pull up in a cheaply tarred parking lot, outside a tall block of flats. The wind rocks Paul's little car. "People from St. Luke's who live here," he says, "used to live near the church in Wynberg in nice cottages with yards and gardens. Group Areas Act." I sigh sympathetically, but I'm thinking: well, we've just been living in the Hawaiian Village Apartments. Through a dark doorway, we move across a windswept quad, cement smelling of vomit and urine. Sand has swept in. Plastic bags rattle. The lifts are broken. "Always," Paul mutters. We go through a door and up five flights of stairs—more vomit and urine smells—then down a hall to a door with a Bible verse on it. "Let your hospitality be unreserved, for thereby some have entertained angels unawares."

Mr. and Mrs. Adams open the door and greet us warmly. They've made tea and we go into their small living room and sit around a coffee table. They pour cups of very strong tea and then add sweetened condensed milk. She goes into the kitchen, and Paul says, indicating the milk—a very special treat opened for you.

I smile and pick up the tea to drink. I nearly gag but sip politely. "What kind of tea is this?" I ask. "Rooibos," Mrs. Adams answers.

Between sips I ask them, do you have children? Mr. Adams moves to a bookshelf and removes a photograph to show me. Fifteen children in front of their Wynberg home. Many of them are professionals in parts of Canada now—Toronto and Calgary, they tell me. I can barely understand their accents, let alone their lives. They have a handicapped child who lives near them, so they can't emigrate, they explain.

I manage to get to the bottom of my cup of tea, and they refill it with even stronger rooibos and add the sweetened condensed milk. I smile politely and pick up my cup. I'm on holy ground—with these saints who hold their faith despite all that has been done to them. Rooibos tea with condensed milk—the cost of discipleship?

As I drain my cup, I resolve to be the best wife ever, to give myself to that calling. We are kept on visitor visas, because we're in the Anglican Church. I can't work or study.

I've been told that all the clergy in this parish have "equally outstanding wives" so I'm determined to be one too. We prepare for E's ordination, and I'm even invited to the pre-ordination retreat. In my letter to my parents, my only comment is about the lemon soufflé—an appropriate offering, I guess, for a household god.

15

My God Wants Me to Grow Up

As the great story tellers know, all life is lived in the details—to paraphrase Flannery O'Connor, mystery is incarnate in the manners of everyday life.[1] Talk of sanctification, holiness, and spiritual depth is meaningless, unless it's dug out of the struggles of life.

Most of us realize there are certain truths more profound than facts. Modernism, with its emphasis on facts, scientific observation, and the rational, has tended to privilege that kind of knowledge: something is truer the more factual it is. Old fashioned Enlightenment ways of knowing (and even of doing theology) had its comforts, as it functioned from the collar up. Simple. All done within the brain.

But there are truer Truths, ones we encounter when we are moved by something profound, mysterious, and deep, in a great painting, symphony, or poem. Great novels often contain more Truth (with a capital T) than do factual accounts. In moving beyond the facts, we are taken to places of profound truth. Some of the greatest truths may be found in a narrative about a person who never lived in a place that never existed, such as Narnia or Middle Earth.

Most of us are deeply invested in some comforting self-deception, and sometimes an experience of truer Truth can shake us from that. We're good at obscuring concepts we use to form beliefs. Presumably David, fornicating with Bathsheba and sending Uriah to be killed in battle, told himself that as king he deserved the women he wanted, or that as commander in chief he had to send someone to the front lines. As long as he could keep himself from "seeing" he could avoid the discomfort of self-contempt, shame, and

1. O'Connor, *Mystery and Manners*.

remorse. Only through Nathan's narrative can he begin to see the deeper truth of who he is and what he has done.[2]

Just as King David begins to see himself more clearly, we sometimes catch a glimpse of our own self-deceptions, seeing how we've chosen certain beliefs. We can see the subplots and how those have led to the overall plot, bringing us greater understanding, closer to "truth in my inmost being," as David tells us God desires.[3]

At this early stage in Cape Town, I'm desperately trying to hold onto a simple story with a magical god who will deliver me. But this god is pushing me to grow up. My main sense of self is as a vicar's wife; I am who I am only in relation to E and his calling. My "professional space" is our home, and it is in the complexity of household relationships that I am forced to struggle with my guilt, my sense of calling, and even my sense of god.

⌖

Madam. My relationship with domestic workers was sacramental—an outward and visible sign of my struggle to be in South Africa. Apartheid (built on the firm foundation of colonial racism) had worked so well, that (outside certain churches) the only contact between black and white was domestic worker/employer.

Over the next few months I was introduced to the lore of domestic help. Complaints were common: "It's so difficult to find good servants nowadays . . . Oh, I know we're supposed to call them domestic workers, but I just can't get used to it . . . My Dora . . ."

You were no longer to call her "girl" but "Rosie" or "Bertha." To maintain respect, she should call you madam or Mrs. Jones. It was common knowledge that you had to pay more for domestic help in Cape Town than in the Orange Free State or Transvaal. A "live in" should get Saturday afternoon off and be paid 40 rand a month plus room and meals. "And make no mistake those meals are not insignificant with my Evelina; have you seen the size she's gotten to be? And I'm sure she takes the leftover roast and potatoes to her children in Nyanga." "Georgina needs bus fare, and I don't know how many times hers has gone up within the last two years."

I don't see Caroline for a few weeks. One afternoon she brings my hardening sheets in off the line as the rain starts. "Thanks, Caroline."

2. 2 Samuel 12:7.

3. Psalm 51.

"Sometimes you see a boy here. It is my brother, Michael. So you know."

"Sure. Do you have other brothers and sisters?"

"One sister. She's bad. She's skully."

"Skully?"

"Skully . . . drink meths and fight. I don't let her know where I stay, or she make trouble for me."

"You're not from here?"

"Montagu . . . 100 miles north; my mother looks after my boy Jocko."

"A son...how old is he?"

"Two years old. Sometime I bring madam a picture."

"Call me Mary Ellen."

"Yes madam. Good bye, madam."

Two months after our arrival, Bishop and Joan Evans, who had moved from the rectory three months earlier, come to visit. "I hear you haven't hired Caroline," Joan said.

"I don't like the idea of having someone work for me just because her skin is darker."

"I don't know how she's surviving. Work is hard to come by, and she has to send money to her mother or her son will starve. She's probably not eating."

A punch to my stomach. "I didn't know that."

So much for my high-minded idealism, my sense that I could live as an American in this country.

Later that day:

"Caroline, I'd like to hire you to work for me two days a week. You probably know better than I what needs to be done." She explained to me that if the hardwood floors were not waxed and polished regularly the fleas would multiply. We were catching them in the nick of time. I watched her on her hands and knees.

Aerogram—October 6, 1975

Caroline just finished cleaning the place and ironing—she does very good work and is quite nice.

In answer to your letter—about living conditions of the blacks—I really couldn't know from living here. From what people say, life in the Cape Peninsula is different from anywhere else in the country—there are hardly any blacks—lots of coloured—meaning a mixture—and English-speaking whites. The culture of the coloured people is radically different from that of the whites—like I hear you get in other part of the country where Lynden-type Dutch are in contact with natives, many of them from the jungle. The situation with the coloured people really varies. Some areas are very nice where they live, and others remind me of the Lummi Indian reservation—slightly run down, yards not kept up, etc. We went to an area where people lived in shanty-shack type places which are fairly grim—they are being torn down and new places built. The difficulties are people like Amos who does the church garden, who lives in one of these shack type places. Though people from the church have made attempts to get him a house—he can't get one because he's not a legal immigrant—a bit like some of the migrant workers. I can't really speak for the rest of the country—I've never been there.

Aerogram—November 30, 1975

In the evening we had the baptism class again—lots of fun—I do find the coloured accent very difficult to understand. I was talking to one lady and she said that her mother had 16 children—14 boys and 2 girls—but ten of the boys died. Seems so foreign.

How can I as a twenty-three-year-old begin to understand what it might be like to be a child growing up in a family with so many children and so much grief?

16

A God Present in the Complexities

FOR DECADES THE ANGLICAN Church in South Africa had been very so-
cially active and Anglo Catholic—what we disparagingly called "high and
dry" and others called "smells and bells." Anglican Church services—open
to all races—were breaking the law constantly. Clergy who protested were
arrested, sometimes put in solitary confinement. Clergy salaries were low,
and families stressed. No wonder clergy burnout levels and alcoholism
rates were high.

Then in the early seventies the Spirit swept through the Anglican
Church in South Africa. The archbishop told us how he'd been reading his
newspaper when the Spirit came upon him. Individual churches, and clergy
of the whole diocese were encouraged by the archbishop to add the Spirit's
joy and power to an exhausting faith. For many, a layer of complexity was
added to their god. For me it reinforced my private god theology.

What I couldn't see then but seems clear now is how little this cost
me. I lived in this gorgeous countryside (not to mention a Mediterranean
climate) in a big house—as one of the good guys, oblivious to my inevitable
complicity in the colonial project. As an American, I could stand apart from
South Africa, although unlike Cape Town's other 1,700 American expats, I
never attended the July Fourth barbecues or other gatherings.

Aerogram: Dec. 3, 1975

*We had a tremendous time at this conference, called by the archbishop
for all the clergy in this area—Monday evening the archbishop spoke and
Tuesday we had several talks and the afternoon free to swim and hike and an*

evening communion service that lasted 2 and a half to 3 hours. The teaching was really tremendous as were the times of praise.

It was a good time for getting acquainted with the other clergy with tremendous variety in the people—all colors, churchmanships, etc. There was a Xhosa couple there called Qabazi—pronounced "'click abazi."

Some clergy were not buying this feel-good stuff. While the archbishop led a time of "singing in the Spirit"—most of the gathering singing "alleluia" or in some prayer language—a man behind me suddenly joined in loudly, "We three kings of orient are . . ."

I feel like I learned a lot about self-acceptance and also some of my attitudes—especially concerning being a wife and mother—really came to the surface. You may be grandparents yet!

I'm very encouraged by my relationship with Caroline (the maid) we're really getting to be friends—for the first time tonight she gave me something— a cantaloupe—usually it's the other way around—(Madam gives to the girl)— and it is so hard for them to get used to a give and take equal relationship. I was so pleased when she gave me that—a real breakthrough! Do you understand? It's so different!

In the evening we had a dinner engagement with some people from the church—a retired colonel and his wife from the British army—very old school. Have I told you that people dress very formally for dinner engagements here? I've been wearing my green formal a lot—the crepe one that I made for Jr. Prom. It's fun to be able to wear those dresses that I thought I'd only be able to wear once or twice. To the theater, people really dress up—my coral formal would be quite normal.

I sit with Colonel and Mrs. Jenkins feeling like I've moved not only around the world, but back 200 years: I'm in a Jane Austen novel, except for the 180-degree view out over the Indian ocean. He is very stiff with a small grey mustache and she fusses around him. They tell me about their nephew is studying at the University of Cape Town and came to see them, but they wouldn't let him in because he was wearing jeans.

Before dinner she says to me, "Do you need to powder your nose?" I look at her. "My nose?" She rubs her hands together, "Wash hands?" Ah, I realize she's telling me to go pee. And I do.

After dinner Colonel Jenkins gets his scrapbook out. From World War II? I wonder. No, it's a record of his outrage—at the Afrikaner nationalists. Glued into this book—clippings of police clubbing demonstrators. He shakes with rage. "Here's when they went after . . ."

Everywhere strange languages, accents, manners. These flimsy blue aerograms make their way to my home and back in four to six weeks.

Aerogram: December 5, 1975

About the phone calls—it costs R2.40—about 2.75 dollars per minute.

I seem to be getting "broody"—that's the word they use for wanting a baby.

Most of the women I'm around have babies; children are their lives. If I look at a baby, people say, "Ah . . . getting broody?" And you don't "get pregnant" here; you "fall pregnant." A fall? A baby would normalize me, give me an outlet for my energy and something that is mine.

As you can imagine the attitude towards US involvement in Angola here is quite different. It's generally thought, and I suppose it's probably true, that if the US doesn't aid the non-communist group—eventually the African situation will be like SE Asia, gradually becoming completely communist. It's hard to see what détente means with the thousands of soviet trained Cuban troops in Angola. Anyhow. Perhaps the pressure put on SA will begin to change some of its internal policies.

I'm sensing people's fear: Rhodesia, SW Africa are buffer zones between South Africa and the communist threat, I'm told. Atrocity tales abound. "Did you hear what happened to the women missionaries in _____?" We've just heard about Salvation Army couple we met on the ship who have been massacred in Rhodesia.

Caroline, who lives in the maid's quarters, is pregnant—second child. It's very common for coloured girls to have four or five illegitimate children—usually cared for by their mothers.

I ask her, "What will you do about medical care?"

"I had Jocko in Montague, but there many babies die."

"Shall I phone around?"

I take her to Groot Schuur Hospital where Chris Barnard performed the first heart transplants. I sit on a wooden bench in the hall while a doctor examines her.

He calls me in while she's still pulling her panties on.

"Your girl is fine, but you don't want this to happen again. You can't get any good work out of them when they're all the time pregnant, multiplying like rabbits. After she delivers, bring her in for an injection—it's like the pill but once a year. You can't trust them to take their pills."

Caroline buttons her blouse. In the car she snorts, "That doctor: he thinks you own me." I realize I don't know Caroline; I had expected her to be grateful to me for taking her to a doctor.

I sign her up for a clinic in Elsie's River, half an hour drive away with no public transport, so I drive her, past people hobbling to the clinic. Sometimes I pull over and offer someone a ride and they are so grateful, "Thank you, madam . . . thank you madam . . ."

Aerogram: March 23, 1976

On Tuesday I took Caroline to a day hospital and then a group of us—4 staff members and I went to Stellenbosch to hear C.K. Barrett, a theologian, speak. He was very good, but afterwards we went to lunch with the two heads of the department of theology at Stellenbosch University. They were very jovial and so bigoted.

I sit in a timbered, whitewashed room. The man sitting next to me asks how my Afrikaans is coming along. "You must learn it," he says. "It is fast becoming one of the world's most important languages." Later I turn to the man on the other side who has heard my accent. "You Americans. You disapprove of apartheid." He smirks. "We would blow the sub-continent to bits sooner than integrate." I look at my plate of elegant food.

Aerogram: June 1, 1976

Wednesday was quite a day—Caroline was cleaning the house and then she said she wasn't sure, but she thought her water had broken. You should have seen us trying to talk about something I know nothing about when we speak different languages. Talk about communication breakdown. Anyhow I took her in to the day hospital and left her. I tried to tidy up the half dozen household chores left from the day before, when the day hospital rang and said that Caroline had just had a little boy—could I come pick her up. So, I went out and got her—the baby only weighed 4 pounds 10 oz. and she had it at 1:15 and was home by 3:30. Boy did I feel responsible with this little person—Caroline and little "Oliver" moved into one of our spare rooms and fortunately Annette who's a midwife came to help and showed me how to do everything since Caroline wasn't feeling so good.

I wanted my god small. Passing a Zulu man as I'm jogging along a suburban street, I say, "Hi." I'm an American and I say "hi" to everyone. He flickers his eyes up to me for a split second: they overflow with hatred. With a jolt in my stomach I realize that he would love to slit my white throat. He doesn't know I'm against apartheid, that in fact I have come to this country to work against apartheid. Well, sort of. I've come to spread the gospel of personal repentance . . . which would end apartheid if it weren't for those horrible Afrikaners. Many English speakers, including me, never come to think of this country as "home."

PART FOUR

17

Whose Side Is God On, Anyway?

IN THE NOVEL, AND in life, it is as the plot thickens that a character may grow. In a course I've taught over the years (*The Plot Thickens: Character Growth in Literature and Life*), we read a number of novels and consider the changes we see in various characters, asking what facilitates their growth. We learn that in a novel, it is through pressure, drama, crisis—that characters begin to see themselves more clearly and grow up. It's not a message that any of us really want to hear, though it rings true from what we know of life, what we read in the scriptures (from a number of traditions), and from the great literature of the world: it is when we go through tough stuff that we grow deeper, stronger, better.

The "plot" of our lives (or the novel) affects the character's understanding of self and others. The quest novel—*Bildungsroman*—often includes both an outer and inner journey. Jane Eyre moves around England some, but her greatest movement is an inward one—toward maturity and strength. Frodo makes his way to the Cracks of Doom, but he also grows wiser. Great novels provide both an inner and outer quest.

Narrative theology has used this idea of narrative arc and character growth to bring a different view of ethical decision-making. Instead of seeing right and wrong as once-off ethical dilemmas—do you tell a lie to shelter the Jew hiding in your attic?—character growth is a cumulative process, parallel to some great characters in novels. The question becomes much bigger—not how do we, in one discrete situation, make the right choice, but how can we nurture our character growth in the same way we see a character evolve under pressure in a novel, gaining understanding of our own true characters?

A great novel is an adult book in the most profound sense—a story that doesn't cut corners or pull a veil over the hard parts. The novel offers stories of dilemmas. We get to know a character more closely than we could know any human being—their thoughts, motives, and actions.

The most remarkable moment in a novel is when the character begins to see herself/himself clearly. In C. S. Lewis's novel *Till We Have Faces,* the protagonist, Orual, tells her story. She shows how badly she has been treated, and how she has lived virtuously. During the telling of the story, she begins to see her own selfishness and blindness.[1]

The character in the present, before emerging into a future, has a chance to look back. What in my past, my family's past—has allowed this character to act this way?

For these characters, and for ourselves, it is often in trauma that character growth can happen. At this stage, my god was a household god, reigning within these walls. And being magical, we'll be okay. Please. But then ... new evidence is introduced: what came to be known as the Soweto riots. And a trip to Rhodesia, which unlike South Africa is not tipping toward, but in the midst of revolution. These make me question my god's priorities.

⌁

We've been in Cape Town about a year, when I'm invited to speak to a women's gathering in northern Rhodesia. I don't think of myself as having a gift for speaking, but I don't know how to say no. I'm wondering if I'm pregnant. I talk them into inviting E too, and they organize a few preaching gigs for him. We know the United States has put a travel advisory out for Rhodesia because of terrorist activity there, so I tell my parents we're going "north" for a couple weeks.

We fly to Johannesburg and check into a Holiday Inn since we fly to Salisbury early the next morning. Television is new to South Africa: very expensive with limited programming, so we don't have one.

Here in our hotel room we turn the set on, but we can't tell what we're watching. It looks like the one and only channel is showing a badly filmed movie—bouncy footage of policemen shooting kids? We puzzle and then turn it off.

At dinner we overhear Americans at the next table: "Did you see what the police were doing? To kids?"

1. Lewis, *Till We Have Faces.*

"And they don't even know enough not to broadcast it all over the country . . ."

We had been watching children mowed down as they protested learning Afrikaans, the language of the oppressor. This was perhaps ten miles from our Holiday Inn. These shootings would come to be called the Soweto Riots and their broadcast into white living rooms would tip South Africa more surely toward revolution.

In the morning we fly to Salisbury. I've met plenty of Rhodesians in South Africa, and most of them are very unhappy—they miss the wildness of their country and reminisce about their nannies. And they worry about family and friends as their country disintegrates.

From them, I've learned that Rhodesia is subject to international sanctions because its prime minister decided not to move toward democracy, instead declaring UDI—a Unilateral Declaration of Independence, so people with Rhodesian passports can't travel except to South Africa and Israel. And the sanctions: old cars languish broken down by the roads since parts can't be replaced. On the plane, broken oxygen masks dangle here and there. They can't be fixed—no parts. No chocolate or raisins either, so we are bearing packets as hostess gifts. We're advised not to get our passports stamped because it might make other countries bar our entrance. One side of the aisle is smoking and the other nonsmoking. I look from my window seat, down at the African bush and the Limpopo River. The great gray greasy Limpopo River, Kipling wrote in his story about the elephant child—a story I told in small libraries in Glacier and Maple Falls. The film of those children in school uniforms, toppling over, plays and replays in my mind.

In Rhodesia people ask us about the Soweto Riots as if we were South African. They feel persecuted—South Africa has its apartheid, shooting school kids for heaven's sake, and they can get all the chocolate and raisins they want! They feel trapped. If you want to leave Rhodesia, you can only take what would be about two hundred dollars with you—not enough to start over in another country. People build lavish sailboats in this landlocked country so that they can transport some portable property out. Why should their lives be so hard? And what about the USA with its segregation, not to mention its Indian reservations?

We head to a small farming community a few hours north of Salisbury. I've never been so tired in my life: the altitude, pregnancy, disorientation?

This country shakes me. I've been asked to speak to a gathering of the Mothers' Union for this whole region.

My wisdom? These are white women who tote guns to protect their children and seldom see their husbands because they're fighting the "terrorists." What would I have said to women settling the American West who are terrified of Indian massacres? I can't tell them that my sympathies tend toward those who want some power and representation, who might well also be called "freedom fighters."

What kind of god would allow the evils of human greed, envy, and colonialism, I ask myself as we sing some "frightfully British" hymn, me sharing the hymnal with a woman who will go back to her farm compound. I get up to speak on the passage they've given me: "Seek ye first the kingdom of god and his righteousness, and all these things will be added unto you."[2] Really?!?

Back in Salisbury, E and I speak at the university, on some edifying Bible passage, and a student invites us over for lunch. We expect a bedsit with pillows on the floor, but instead it's an enormous mansion with grounds and servants, even a footman standing uniformed in an empty room, another polishing a Bentley in the driveway. They address this raggedy student as "master." His parents have managed to get Swiss passports, so they don't live here, nor in their rural home a hundred miles away. He's a fine Christian.

We see an albino man in a kind of jail cage, and we're told his flesh is so valuable for black magic that he has to be protected or he would be killed, chopped up, and sold.

People offer to show us the countryside, so we drive along roads called strip roads, with two strips of asphalt. I'm sitting in front, so I don't get carsick, but that gives me the job of looking out for landmines. "Look for any disturbances in the dirt between the asphalt strips. That could be a landmine." Years later I tell this story and Andrew says, "Where was I?" "Oh, I was pregnant with you." "Mom!"

A Cape Town friend has asked us to visit the farm where she grew up, and I travel back in time a hundred years. The Traceys are well educated Christian people who bought these thousands of acres fifty years before; they have raised their four daughters here. Their house consists of an enormous main room with a high thatched roof: I look up before lunch and see spiders and bats. Each corner has a bedroom. The kitchen area is largely outdoors.

2. Matthew 6:33.

Nothing on this farm is fancy and as we walk around we can see why: there are literally hundreds of workers and their families, plus clinics, elementary schools for children. The Traceys own all the land, and that can't be right, I think. But Mr. Tracey tells us that the land doesn't support small farming. We walk along a red dirt road and natives run out to look at us—they've been told there's an American, no doubt—as the great red African sun begins to set. The Traceys could make more money raising tobacco but they have a conscience about raising something that kills. After the meal, Mr. Tracey reads to us from a well-worn Bible. He pulls a card out of a file on the table and prays at length for the family listed on it.

There's a warning against night travel because of attacks. Mr. Tracey says God has called them to make this trip weekly to lead a Bible Study in a nearby town. Understanding the risks, do we want to go with them? Yes, E says, though I would have preferred the spiders and bats. Three women open their Bibles, while one cowers in the corner wringing her hands. Driving back to the farm, Mrs. Tracey tells us that she lived through the Mau Mau revolution in Kenya and has not been right since.

Some twenty years later I hear that the Traceys' farm has been seized to be divided up and they have been killed. Not by the people living on the farm but by others who say Robert Mugabe gave them permission to take the land.

❧

I reel back to Cape Town, shaken. We tell ourselves we are working for change, but do we really want it? The voices of those Rhodesian women—brittle with fear, loneliness, and grief—echo in my mind. Being barricaded in compounds, feeling trapped, losing family members: previews of the next installment here. The images of young people dropping in their school uniforms haunt me. Why am I here?

Whose side is god on, anyway? The Afrikaner nationalists in South Africa knew god had called them to keep the race clean and white. The World Council of Churches and the Anglican Church believed god had called them to end apartheid. Could god be god of both the Rhodesian settlers and the freedom fighters?

If god is on the side of the freedom fighters, where would that leave me and the other good people with great personal faith I know? Can my god be trusted to protect me or is he distracted by all these needs?

Back in Cape Town, I go to worship services, smile into coloured faces. I go to every church service, attend church meetings, sing in the choir, visit people who seem a little lonely. I lead a weekly Bible study for women twice my age and serve tea to a group three to four times my age who meet after morning communion from the 1662 *Book of Common Prayer*. These women have lived in South Africa for decades, some were born here, and yet they speak of England as "home."

People are so nice, but I will always be "the American" and the "vicar's wife." I'm beyond loneliness . . . I long for a mother to look after me, someone to keep me safe. I see glimpses of how a person might think they're doing good but end up doing evil . . . how can we possibly tease out what is done for god?

E and I go to see my ob-gyn—Martin, as he tells us to call him. I write to my parents that he was junior partner to Sir John Peal in England who was the gynecologist to the Queen!

Aerogram: August 8, 1976

He let us listen to the baby's heartbeat and I say to E afterwards, "Wasn't that exciting!!!!??" and he says rather nonchalantly, "Well, yes. Mostly it was interesting" (making it sound purely scientific). For the rest of the day, everyone we saw, E said, "Guess what!!!!! We heard the baby's heartbeat!" What a guy!

What a guy. Isn't it funny? Such a scientific, rational person god has given me, not to mention the British stiff upper lip. Just exactly what I need to counter my emotional ups and downs. I read books about childbirth—it's called labor for a reason, I read—it's hard work and it's misleading to call it pain. This book was written by a man, but I'm desperate to believe him. I swim daily and practice my breathing: this will be a piece of cake.

We move into Christ Church House, and Caroline moves with us into a room by our washing lines. She cleans for us two days a week. Part of my calling is to make busy Christ Church House "home." We have little money, so I decorate with carpet and paint leftovers, sew place mats and cushions.

I am an excellent vicar's wife: never ending cups of tea or ersatz (chicory) coffee, scones (or cookies!), and meals. All served with a winning, patient smile: who knows how a gracious hostess might tenderize someone for the magic that may happen in the holiest of holies—E's study? Our lounge functions as a waiting room—I look in and there is a nun and a desperate looking middle-aged white man, chain smoking. A few years later, Andrew learns to work this, moving from person to person with his favorite books.

When labor starts I can't believe anything could hurt so much. We drive to Mowbray Maternity Hospital and they give me a pain killer which makes me so disoriented I can't figure out where I am or why they are torturing me. I beg E, "Can't you get them to put me to sleep?" He says, "They already gave you something." What I am trying to say is, "They put down dogs who are in pain . . . Why can't they put me down?" Nurses in training come in and out: "Is this her first?"

Finally, Martin swoops in for the delivery; he and E discuss some recent scientific discovery while I'm pushing as hard as I can . . .

Andrew is born, and I hold him: bowled over by mother love: I will protect this little one . . .

When we get home, the kitchen is full of casseroles, salads, and baked goods. I nurse and greet people who feel this is their baby since I am the vicar's wife. Dozens of beautiful little sweaters and blankets fill Andrew's shelves.

He's only two weeks old, and I put him in his crib to sleep, and move to have a nap in our bedroom. E takes the dog out and I hear a noise on the landing. I nearly put my earplugs in and roll over but then think . . . no. I open the door and there is a young coloured man standing on the landing near Andrew's room—"No," I shriek and "How dare you?" and chase him out of the house and down the street screaming at him. "You might have been knifed," people say. "You should have phoned the police." I think (but can't say as a good minister's wife) . . . I didn't want him arrested; I wanted to kill him . . . for getting near my baby.

Can I protect what needs protecting here?

18

Hoping for an Attentive God

INITIALLY MOTHERHOOD NARROWED MY world to that eight-inch gap between my baby's eyes and mine: my arms as a circle encompassing all that mattered. My narrative would need to be retold as I was broken open by childbirth—motherhood's only guarantee. That person who could ride along a strip road looking for disturbances in the soil, with a baby in utero, was gone forever.

My new narrative centered on my fierce desire to protect my baby. I tried not to think of the other women living in coloured or black areas who felt this way, but couldn't protect their little ones, couldn't take a plane away from their lives. Where was god in this? And the guilt: my childbirth was not fun, but completely different from Caroline's.

As a new mother, I want my mom. Casting around for comfort and support, I somehow believe my mom will make everything right. If I can just add her presence to my story, I will be fine. Some time before we had made plans to meet my parents in England a few months after the baby's birth. Someone in the congregation loans us a bungalow and car in Poole; someone gives us a basket to carry the baby.

I am desperate. As a vicar's wife, I must live only for others, this endless stream of parishioners who drop by for tea and a chat, as well as people who spend nights or weeks with us because the parish needs somewhere for them to stay. People have the same problems in South Africa that they have everywhere—drugs, infidelity, financial difficulties, illness. And on top of those, the pressures of the deteriorating social/political situation.

And fear. Just before we fly from Cape Town, I hold Andrew at a clergy gathering and hear someone say, "When the revolution comes, nobody is going to ask—before they slit our white throats—how we felt about apartheid." Every few days the lights flicker out, and people look at each other. Sabotage. How much power does the African National Congress have? Where is your passport?

"You'll find when you leave South Africa and arrive in Europe, you'll feel the relief. Non-apartheid air is easier to breathe," people told me. That first week, before my parents arrive, E sleeps all day while I push Andrew in his push chair. No one knows me; I don't have to feel guilty all the time. I walk along, pushing my baby like any other mother.

Under these gray skies and green trees, I hits me: I can never go back and stay in that pressure cooker. I sob when I think of translating while I'm shopping, opening the door to beggars, bargaining for vegetables and fruit, decorating on a shoe string. I am twenty-five and wearied to death of being public property—the vicar's wife.

E's work is so important, since he is now in charge of Christ Church. For months he's come home and dropped into bed, gotten up early to prepare his talks and visit people. Believing as I do in a god who calls all the shots (though often pulling my strings through my husband whom I've been called to), I have no agency to say no.

I love this baby so much: he is indeed the most beautiful being to enter my life. But I need a mother who will take the baby and shush him, hold him, and say, "Go and take a nap, Mary Ellen. I'll look after this little one."

E and I decide (with eager support from my mom and dad) to look for jobs while we're in England. We frantically pull all our Church of England strings, telling old seminary profs that we have committed for three years in Cape Town, and we've done two, and so we will go back for one more. E says, "We want something a bit more mainstream." We see an old prof at Oxford, who mumbles, "It's a shame. I would have had something for you last year, but not now."

I can't go back and stay in South Africa. I can't. I hold my baby, look at my parents. I can't. Please god.

I don't see that what I'm longing for doesn't exist. Gray-green Bellingham; parents who want to let me rest: all fantasy. Any parish in the UK would be boring, depressing. I'm longing for a god who makes life easy for nice people, who guarantees safety. I don't want to grow up.

Near the end of our time in England, we visit friends near York. E and I decide to go to the evening service at St. Michael le Belfry, a church next to York Minster. My parents offer to watch Andrew.

We drive into town, park near the Cathedral, and go into the church, where 500 people have gathered. We don't know anyone there: it feels good to be anonymous, to follow the familiar service, sing some old hymns, come choruses.

During the Eucharist, we go forward for bread and wine, and then return to our balcony seat and kneel to pray. A woman gets up and whispers something to the priest, who nods. The music stops as she goes to the microphone and speaks. "There's a couple here tonight from far away . . . a place that is hot. It's a place that feels very pressurized and stressful. You feel exhausted, spent. You just want to leave that place, to get away. God says this to you—go back and be there . . . your time there is not done. You still have much to learn. Go back." Half way through her words I start to weep, and then to bawl. E is looking stunned. We sit in the pew and the singing resumes . . . and then we get up and slip out into the darkness.

We have no choice. My parents don't understand why we've changed our minds. This miraculous "word" from a magical god was obnoxiously obvious because there was nothing else we could have heard. I couldn't have said to anyone, let alone god, "I'm scared and tired and lonely . . ."

As a mother I want only to escape and protect, but this god we've promised to obey wants us back in South Africa for a few more years. Aye, aye, sir. Whatever you say, sir. No wonder pictures of me at this stage of life show me looking lost and serious. I can only put one foot in front of the other.

I start running, seven or eight miles, daily if I can hand off the baby. When I pass a group of black builders they stop work and roar with laughter, calling and hooting to each other as if a white woman running is the funniest thing in the world. I run on.

I cook, bake, sew, visit, decorate, lead Bible studies, sing in the choir, play in the parish orchestra, facilitate groups. If god has forced me back here, I'm going to use this time. I open myself more fully to the beauty of the wild landscape—hiking several times a week, doing day long bike rides with friends.

↭

Aerogram—October 1, 1977

This African choir is performing next door today—sound so lovely and different—they're such nice people. Wish you could hear them.

Funny situation here—the big luxury houses are selling for almost noth-
ing—houses ritzier than any of the Edgemoor ones (marble staircases, chan-
deliers, swimming pools) selling for R30,000 to R35,000. People don't want to
invest much because of future uncertainty and they're the sort of places that
you'd need a fleet of servants to run!

Here within the systemic evil of apartheid, even the devil presents himself in household issues. A woman living in a beautiful home in
Bishopscourt cannot keep domestic help because her maid's quarters are
haunted: a new person moves in and the first night, they are thrown off the
bed and flames ripple around the walls. She flies in a powerful sangoma
from Soweto, but he refunds his fee and says he can't do anything with
this one. Someone suggests she phone the Anglican church and a couple of
Oxbridge-educated clergy dig out the service for exorcism in *The Book of*
Occasional Services. They sprinkle holy water on the walls and pray in the
name of Jesus. Problem solved. We get phone calls every few months, "I
hear you do exorcisms."

Where is the true evil here?

Aerogram—November 17, 1977

Last Saturday we had a parish barbecue with several hundred people. It
was super to see all the kids of different races play soccer together. After dinner
the orchestra played, and everyone sang.

I've had to ask Caroline to leave since some of her friends have been
leaving the gate from the yard into the street open and Andrew plays out there.

I hear shrieks and bottles being broken from Caroline's room, and next
morning she arrives late with a cut above her eye. "My brother's friends,
they got so drunk." Twice that week one of her friends leaves the gate open
and I find Andrew out in the street.

"Who's leaving the gate open?"

"It won't happen again," she says.

More bottles, the gate left open. Mary, a local "live in" speaks to me:
"Madam, Caroline has gotten in with the skully, her sister's crowd. She
shouldn't be around children. They would hurt them."

I ask Caroline to come in and she stares at the kitchen table. How can
I make her homeless? "I'm sorry, Caroline, but you must leave."

She doesn't look up and the next day she is gone.

OMG

Aerogram: May 9, 1978

I've really slipped in my letter writing enthusiasm—I guess because I realize I'm going to see you fairly soon. Can hardly wait.

Several friends have raised money for me to take Andrew to visit my parents. I'm so excited I can hardly sleep.

On Wednesday I went to Berkeley House, the local nursery school where Andrew will go, and gave the kiddies a violin demonstration. In one class of three to four-year-olds there were twenty kinds, six of whom were the Rosenkovich sextuplets. Imagine having six at once! Three boys and three girls all dressed much the same.

I fly from Cape Town to Vancouver with fifteen-month-old Andrew and spend six weeks with my parents. I've dreamed of this as the answer to my exhaustion, but I'm responsible for Andrew, getting up early with him so my parents can sleep. People ask me about South Africa, but clearly have no idea where it is or what's happening there. Life in America seems disappointing and superficial: I find myself relieved to be heading back to Cape Town.

Aerogram: August 27, 1978

The flight back to SA wasn't too bad. When I got back to the house, there were bouquets of flowers and home-baked food. Peter and Lindy picked me up and arranged supper and then Pandy wandered the house finding all the old toys and his room, etc. (and also wandering through E's study looking for him). Anyhow Andrew went to bed and I went to church—it was awfully good to be there—got such a warm welcome—I don't know . . . it seems that people here really thoroughly enjoy the worship services and that's refreshing.

I bring a bunch of books back from America for a member of our staff team. They include Flannery O Connor's *Everything that Rises Must Converge*. When I hand them to Sid, he smiles and opens one of them and shows me: it's Steve Biko's banned book. "I didn't want to tell you in case you got nervous and they sensed it."

19

A Pushy God

I HAVE BEGUN TO realize the limits of an American god, who could be placed on the mantle along with other trinkets. No pressing concern for the poor or oppressed. Services were dull and sermons of the "I'm okay, you're okay" school.

My South African god, highlighted against the backdrop of a fight against evil, was intense and demanding. This god wanted more than my civility and comfort. Yet, within my marriage, my role as minister's wife, what could I do?

Our beliefs about ourselves and god are warped mirrors, reflecting back truth and falsehood. Still, one of life's great callings is to reach toward truth. It's a demanding task, one we're unlikely to bother with when we're comfortable. I think of Eustace in C. S. Lewis's *The Voyage of the Dawn Treader*, who finds himself turned into a dragon. His scales must be clawed off before he can become who he really is.[1]

To rewrite a fairy-tale into a complex narrative is the work of years.

We move from the fairy-tale by shaping a new story, moving to a narrative more multifaceted and novel-like. *Middlemarch, War and Peace, The Lord of the Rings* echo life—seething as they do with inner and outer journeys, surprises, conflicts within characters and their worlds, plots and subplots, and endless opportunities for growth.

My household god begins to crack one Christmas.

---

1. Lewis, *The Voyage of the Dawn Treader*.

Instead of being a bright spark of jollity and warmth in the darkness, as it is in northern realms, Christmas in Cape Town came during school vacation, wedding season, and high summer. Most locals went to church, ate a cool meal, and went to the beach. From our first Christmas, I tried to counter what seemed so foreign by capturing some Christmas magic: making calico ornaments, gingerbread cookies, a nativity scene.

For a couple of years, I did a big Christmas dinner at Christ Church house. We would invite a few friends, but the main purpose of the dinner was to provide an English feast for some of the British expats in the church. I did it because I was a good vicar's wife.

Growing up in western Washington State I'd experienced plenty of depressing darkness. But here I was supposed to re-create some magic I never experienced myself: an olde English Christmas, nurtured in World War I or World War II when the world was so dark that an orange in the toe of a stocking, the light of carol singing, and a cup of wassail was a delight. This magic in the heat of a Cape Town summer day! From November I'd have nightmares of opening the front door and there are Colonel and Mrs. Buckle and I haven't taken the turkey out of the freezer.

Sewing beautiful little pincushions, glasses cases, cosmetic bags, and wrapping them to go beside each plate along with a Christmas cracker. And then the cooking . . . 90 degrees out, Christmas carols wafting from the church across the street and I'm doing roast potatoes in the outstanding way I've been taught: you take the turkey out and turn up the oven to 450 degrees while you boil the potatoes just a bit, not too much—they must be firm—and then scratch each of them all over with a fork and put a pan with oil and dripping in the oven to come up to temperature, and then add the potatoes and stir occasionally while they become perfectly brown and crunchy. Meanwhile you finish the other veggies . . . Brussel sprouts of course and beans and peas . . . the number of veg is like a Michelin star rating system on meals . . . roast and three veg, but the potatoes will get me extra points. And then check the pudding—a recipe from a woman whose parents own an inn in Cornwall known for its Christmas puddings. I'd made it a couple months ago so it could soak up its flavors, and now it's been steaming for a couple hours. The brandy butter is made and in the fridge and the gravy ingredients out for when I lift the turkey and start to work with the drippings . . . I won't have to salt it since I'm dripping my own sweat into it!

I look at the table again—Di and Pat, Colonel and Mrs. Buckle, Chris, E, Andrew, and I . . . and Gilbert . . . I like him because he calls me Mary Ellen, not "madam." He is Xhosa and works on the lobster boats. I've invited him to join us for lunch.

I hear the final carol from the morning's fifth service—"Hark the Herald Angels Sing" . . .

And head back to the kitchen . . .

There is a knock at the door and the Buckles come into the living room, he in a suit and she in a lovely spring frock. They hobble into the living room and take their glass of sherry. Have you heard from your daughter? No, not yet but maybe later today . . . time zones are complicated since she's in Malaysia. I sniff sympathetically—their only child who seldom writes or calls. Pat and Di, carrying Andrew, come in from church. E walks in exhausted, and Chris with her dog, Woodstock. In the corner of the living room is a very sparse pine Christmas tree, bought from the local Christian bookstore, decorated with handmade ornaments—red and green calico prints sewn into patchwork stars and lions and lambs. Such a wonderful image of Christmas peace, these small stuffed creatures hanging on this most un-Christmas like of trees, poor thing, that was never meant to grow in this climate. Would the lion and the lamb ever lie down together, in this setting, ripe for revolution?

Sipping our sherry in the heat, E gazes blankly. Christmas eve services until late last night and then five services this morning in the heat. Too many "Happy Christmases" and "great sermon, vicar" greetings. All he wants is a nap, but here we are. One more sherry and we'll all lie down, lambs and lions or not.

I go to finish the meal, ask E to carve, and then realize Gilbert is not here yet. Africans are known to be late, and I've tried to hint that we need him on time. I excuse myself and run out the large oak door of the thick-walled stucco house. There are nights when I'm so thankful for all that thick stucco and that heavy door which—I tell myself—would keep all but the most violent marauders out.

The sunlight is blinding. After all, this is midsummer. I go out the gate, across the quiet street, and in through the St. Anne's gate toward the small servant's room where Gilbert lives. The door is open, and people are laughing, spilling out the door, raising glasses of something, speaking in Xhosa, of which I know only one or two words.

As I walk up they quieten a bit. "Happy Christmas," I say brightly. Yes, happy Christmas they say in their yes madam voices. Gilbert appears from the depths, a big smile on his face. He says in his normal voice, "Yes, Happy Christmas. You see I have company. I am so glad."

"I'd hoped you were coming to dinner with us."

"Yes. But now these are here. Unless you'd like us all to come."

For a moment I see all of us parading across to Christ Church House, opening the front door, abandoning the dining room table, and scattering into the stoep and the garden, eating and talking . . . some new joy, some sense of possibility, some new life rises in me.

I think of E's face. He'd shake his head knowingly—what will the wife think of next?!—and then drop his voice to tell me how important this is for the Buckles and others and we can't introduce any more chaos into their lives.

"Just a minute," I say. "I'll run and ask." Through the heat and sun of a Christmas Day, it doesn't occur to me that I'm like a child asking permission. Or maybe I could run down the street, hop on a train, and go to the beach. I imagine myself getting to the sand, stripping off my proper shoes and my homemade Liberty cotton dress and dashing into the waves that sweep me off my feet.

I open the door and step into the cool darkness of the house. "What is going on?" E demands. I don't even get the "you cute, crazy little woman" look. "Ridiculous. It would completely spoil the day. I'll start carving." He turns toward the kitchen.

I run back across the street.

"Maybe another time," I say to them. "Have a lovely Christmas." As I turn I can hear their voices resume reality—laughter, bantering—and I make my way back across the street to finish the nostalgia farce for people who will never see a new South Africa.

I join the frightfully British group in Christ Church house. There were three main political parties at the time—all white. One was the Progressive Party of people like Alan Paton and Nadine Gordimer. Another more centrist one was the United Party. And then the evil party of the Afrikaners—the Nationalists. People spoke truth when they said, "Oh, the English-speaking whites. If they have become citizens so they can vote, they talk Progressive Party, vote United Party, and thank God for the Nationalists."

Despite the stirrings of this other god calling me to grow up, I needed my intensely personal household god. Disappearances, power outages, bugged phones, and I held my babies closer. Our parish flew in speakers from England who were part of the Charismatic movement, their pasty white skin portending their oblivion about South Africa: they focused on personal sin, conversion, and experience of the Spirit.

Surely it wasn't too much to ask god to protect me. Our friends had weighed leaving but chosen to stay and work toward and in a new South Africa. And as a vicar's wife—well, fear would imply that I didn't have enough faith.

<p>

Aerogram—July 16, 1979

Sorry I missed a week again, but it's been very busy. Fortunately, at the last minute someone gave us air tickets to Pretoria so rather than driving 27 hours we've been able to fly for 2. We left CT on Thursday, after a great flurry of activity. This huge conference—SACLA—4,000+ people was arranged so that people could stay with the locals in Pretoria.

SACLA—the South African Christian Leadership Assembly. Registration for an Ashcroft was easy, but they'd forgotten there would be huge long lines of M's and N's, with all the Zulu and Xhosa names. SACLA was a life-changing experience for many, since apartheid so effectively kept races apart—we worshiped together and heard talks on a future for the country. A number of key movements were born there, including the Crossroads SACLA clinic in Cape Town.

The conference itself was super. I found myself thinking—in most countries one has only really denominational barriers to contend with in the church and perhaps churchmanship ones—i.e. charismatic, social action, evangelical, etc. Here you have not only those but very real cultural (English Afrikaans), racial (black, white, coloured Indians), tribal (Zulu Xhosa, Sotho, etc., etc.) not to mention language [differences]. We sang songs in English, Afrikaans, Zulu, Xhosa, and Sotho. Some people are highly educated/others not at all. Besides these there are years of misunderstanding, distrust, bitterness, and fear on all sides. It was absolutely remarkable to see all these barriers broken down in Christ! I think the best talk was by an American guy named Ron Sider on "word and deed." All in all, it was a very eye-opening time and very helpful as far as church strategy here.

OMG

Desmond Tutu's talk inspires me, and I'm beginning to see that faith can't be private; we need each other. My god, I could see from this conference, demands much more than my personal piety.

PART FIVE

20

Trying to Please God

WE ARE CALLED TO do something—I had seen government abuses, but being shoulder to shoulder with people at the conference, had shown me that, yes, we need to follow god in a new way. But I'm pregnant and societal expectations of who does what—the man does the intellectual, public work, while the little woman decorates and cooks—limited not only what I could do, but what I could imagine doing.

Narrative studies underline the idea that we may have limited templates for our stories. As Virginia Woolf points out in *A Room of One's Own*, women's friendships were rarely (if ever) written about up to the era in which she lived.[1] It's not that people were forbidden from writing about them—the template simply did not exist. Or, Carolyn Heilbrun points out that, in her mysteries, Dorothy L. Sayers is the first writer to portray a woman making an important decision about something other than courtship or marriage.[2] These "lacks"—these holes within the available stories, are invisible to us until pointed out.

My narrative line at this stage could only allow me action within my home so as a character my agency was limited. But god is calling beyond personal faith: how about a household response to god's call?

1. Woolf, *A Room of One's Own*, 82.
2. Heilbrun, *Writing a Woman's Life*, 55–58.

Aerogram—March 1, 1980

We've been meeting on Mondays for supper—we, being the people who live in our house and St. Anne's across the street—it's very nice. Works out awfully well baby sitter wise because Andrew considers Di and Sid and Lyn and Chris to be his best buddies, so I can go out with E without any problems.

Christ Church sits on a corner next to a large old house called St. Anne's, owned by the church. Christ Church House, the rectory, sits directly across the street. After SACLA we decide to start an intentional community, with Ivan, who is starting a clinic in Crossroads, Di, who is a midwife in a 'coloured' area, Chris, who is starting the South African hospice movement, and Pat and Claire, who work for the church.

Aerogram—March 10, 1980

Ivan Thoms has moved into our laundry room and they're putting bigger windows in and repainting and carpeting etc. He's starting this clinic at Crossroads (well known squatter camp). Quite nice to have a doctor in the house—specialty pediatrics.

When Steve is born, we know so many doctors and midwives that they all show up for his birth; the nursing sister asks if there's anyone else we'd like to invite.

I also decide that there must be a way for me to have a meaningful interracial relationship, so I decide that the way to do that is to establish an alternative relationship with domestic help.

Aerogram—March 17, 1980

Well our five day a week char starts Monday, so our life may become more organized. Her name's Mable and she's a delightful, huge Xhosa woman. She comes to Christ Church sometimes. On Sunday I was sitting chatting to about 8–10 blacks after the service and Stephen cried so I started to nurse him and they all gathered round for close inspection because normally here black women nurse in public and white women never. The Xhosa word for nursing is pronounced "ntza ntza"—sounds like a baby drinking.

Mable looks at me. "You crazy," she says. "Eight rands a day to clean. In Guguletu they brag to get two fifty." Stretching a thick arm along the back of the antique love seat, and crossing vast legs where they narrowed slightly at the ankles. "Why so much, Mary?"

That's it. I want to hug her . . . not madam or miss: she calls me Mary. Was a bonus of R5.50 five rand a day too much for that?

"Christ Church House is huge and six of us live here. Besides me and E, Andrew, and baby Stephen . . . you've met Ivan, who's starting the clinic at Crossroads, and Di, who delivers babies in Elsie's River. And Pat.

"We despise the government and apartheid, and nobody should get paid what domestic workers get here. We settled on what seems a fair wage. We want you to be honest with us and we'll be honest with you . . . you know, if you feel irritated about something, let us know, and we'll do the same."

Steve whimpers and starts to wail. Mable heaves herself from the love seat. "Come little man-child." She lifts him onto her enormous bosom, swaying and humming a Xhosa song. He shuts his mouth in mid-cry, eyes staring into hers.

"Most of the time, I like to look after the kids myself. He's probably hungry. I'll take him."

"You not hungry, no little man-child: you want to dance with Mable."

I unbutton my blouse. "I'll take him," I say, reaching up.

Mable swings round and peers through her thick glasses at my insignificant breast. She hands Steve to me. "Very pretty, very pretty." She strokes my white flesh. "You give him ntza-ntza."

I ask her to show me how to carry a baby African-style with a blanket holding Steve on my back. She tries and then shakes her head sadly, "I'm sorry, Mary, but you are the wrong shape. Too white. Not enough breasts and butt."

Aerogram March 24, 1980

On Wednesday I went with Mable out to Guguletu for lunch—they've started a lunch club for the old agers there. To celebrate many wore their tribal dress—absolutely fantastic! Afterwards we visited a nursery school. All the little black kiddies gathered round Andrew touching him—poor kid!! He nearly leapt into my arms. Afterwards we went to Mable's house. She's done it up so nicely. We had tea and chatted—it was super.

On Thursday we took some toys out to a day care center in Guguletu—super to have the contact there. I must say—having Mable with us is like doing cross cultural research all the time—her expressions, language and ideas are fascinating. She was telling me yesterday about all her names and who's allowed to call her what in their custom—also about her marriage—all arranged by parents when she was 16. Very enjoyable learning from her.

Mable is supposed to work Monday to Friday, nine to four. But she finds it hard to get on the bus from Guguletu and then misses her train in Rondebosch. By 9:45 I hear her singing as she sways up the street.

Sometimes she cleans, but often she finds some obscure piece of silver and spends two hours polishing it, showing it to me gleefully. When visitors arrive, she sidles up to me: "Mary, show her the dish."

One day Mable comes to work in an apron with safety pins along one seam and a torn pocket. I don't remember her wearing it before. She shakes her head. "Not good in umfundisi house, Mary, for me to look this way. This is what I want." She pulls a grubby piece of paper out of her pocket. Pink and white check; XXX outsize.

I walk two blocks up to the main road and go into Teales with its fancy twinsets—imported from England for the "madams" and racks of apron overalls. There is one size medium, two large, and then outsized ones. I pick out one for Mable.

Aerogram—April 12, 1980

I'm really feeling so tired—sleepy from broken nights and getting to bed late and up too early, and also tired of the pressure of doorbells, phones, entertaining, etc., etc., etc. E's feeling very tired what with being acting rector, etc. Don't get me wrong it's all highly satisfying and fulfilling and we love the people and the church and the place; but the combination of too much pressure and not enough sleep is a bit much, really, after a while. One needs a good break to catch up.

I organize vacations in parishioners' beach cottages—wild places without running water or electricity. I am exhilarated by the landscape but exhausted by washing heavy terry towel diapers by hand and hanging them on a line while the sea roars.

Almost daily Mable brings up the topic of my husband's underpants. "He needs blue or green or purple," she shakes her head as she folds his white ones. "White ones no good," she frowns as if these might have dire consequences.

"But those are what he likes . . ."

I begin to find his underpants stuffed with the silver polish or the toilet cleaner. A month later, I find myself in Woolworths buying him two packets of blue, green, and purple underpants.

Aerogram—January 1, 1981

Well we got a bicycle on Monday—found a super Peugeot for ½ price in the paper—with the bike seat on, A and I have had some super rides—I feel so happy to be on a bicycle again—we got a lovely helmet for A and he absolutely loves it!

I bike Andrew to his preschool past the busy commuter train station. Most mornings someone has spray-painted on the wall—FREE NELSON MANDELA. By the time I bike back half an hour later someone has spray-painted it out. There must be anti-graffiti crews all over the city.

Christ Church House has no central heating, and in the middle of winter it could be in the forties or fifties both outside and in. I wear a beautiful Irish fisherman's sweater almost daily. "Mary, you do not look nice in that sweater. It looks very bad on you."

I'm surprised. "Well, I like it, Mable. It was given to me by my great aunt. And it's so warm." She looks down.

A few weeks later I cross the landing where Mable is folding clothes. "Mary, never will you wear this sweater again." She holds up the sweater, transformed into toddler size.

"You must have washed it with the nappies!"

"Yes, I think that is what happened." She looks down with a slight smirk. "It was not good on you."

There is no question who is in charge of the house. All my longings for an honest friendship . . . I could not say no to her.

I begin to dread this pink and white apparition, waddling from the living room, blowing dust off a book, picking up a toy and carrying to the stoep. If I decide to assert some authority as her employer and call her to do something, she doesn't hear me. She plays with Andrew, and at Stephen's slightest whimper she appears, lifting him from me. Sometimes when she changes his diaper she picks him up and kisses his penis in a reverential way: "Little man-child . . ." Then she pulls him onto her back, knotting a blanket to hold him, she sways out of sight.

In January I decide I must tell Mable to leave.

My mouth is dry. I make coffee. "Mable, I need to talk to you."

She lowers herself into a chair, takes a noisy sip of coffee, adds three teaspoons of sugar, stirs it, and takes a bite of her cookie.

I swallow, trying to get up my nerve to tell her. "Mable . . ."

"So you finally notice," she says.

I look at her blankly.

"Come on, Mary," she grins. "It comes in three weeks."

A baby? I search her enormous bulk and see no extra bumps.

"Mary. That's why you wanted to talk to me."

"Well. I wondered when you want to stop working."

"I will work until my time and then stop off work for two weeks."

"Mable. Ivan, Pat, and Di are moving out, and so we will not be able to afford so much help. We will have to let you go. Do you think I can look after this big house?"

Mable looked at me. "Mary, you will work very hard. I am sad."

On her last day Mable brings her children with her . . . we watch seven naked bodies, five brown and two white, glisten as they run through the sprinkler, shrieking in Xhosa and English. Before she leaves she wraps her huge arms around me, her children watching. Keep in touch . . . and bring the new baby.

I close the door with relief. So much for friendship.

The community moves on, and Mable moves out. Is crossing racial divides even possible in this apartheid world?

We tell only a few people—the rector, the archbishop, a few close friends—that E feels that it is time to move. We check out a church in Natal because the archbishop suggests it; hear from a church in St. Paul beginning a search. The bishop of the Yukon phones from Yellowknife, and there's an opening at a church in Cambridge. A church in Cleveland is looking for an associate. E applies for all of them. I pray desperately to my magical god. It's been six years . . . can you get me out of here?

⊷

Two weeks later, Vivian arrives. The doorbell rings, and before me is a *Vogue* model. She wears a low waisted brick red dress with a silk scarf knotted at her neck and a green hat slanted over one eye.

Graceful and lean, she removes her sunglasses. "I'm Vivian," she says, extending her hand.

"I'm Mary Ellen . . . Ashcroft."

"I'll call you Ms. Ashcroft. Let me look around and see if I can do this house in one day a week."

Twenty minutes later she comes back into the kitchen. "This is a big house. It will take me three hours to do a thorough job on the kitchen and the rest of the house in four. I would like five rand, plus bus fare to and from Nyanga."

I nod. What a relief. Someone I don't have to try to be friends with or worry about.

Once a week Vivian arrives, puts on a black shift, and works. Our conversations: "We need more toilet bowl cleanser." Or "The return fare has gone up from R1.45 to R1.75."

Aerogram—May 31, 1981

Great business here because of the 20th anniversary of So. Africa being a "republic." All the people who are anti the government are protesting in some way or another—flag burnings, black protest sashes, etc. Because the people who are patriotic here are so fervently so, and the oppressed are so extremely oppressed—feelings are running very high. I'm sure you can understand having read The Covenant. There's a holiday here, commemorating the "Day of the Covenant" which is referred to scornfully as "the day of the government." It reminds me of the anti-Vietnam war feelings but at a much more grassroots and emotional level. On Wed. all the schools were supposed to have a "Republic Day Assembly"—national anthem and patriotic speech—and at many of the English-speaking schools, the principals just let school out. Never a dull moment!

We had a fabulous time at Betty's Bay with Stuart and Ca. We went on Thursday afternoon and came back on Sat. On the way there, Steve discovered "scenery"—spent the trip, an hour or so, leaning forward in his seat looking out the windows. And shouting "cloud" "trees" "rainbows." On the way there, there were fabulous rainbows over the mountains and the sea looked placid enough to sail on. We had such a super time—went for long walks on the beach—the weather was perfect, but we were almost always the only people on the beach. On the Friday morning, Ca and I left E and Stuart and the boys jumping in the dunes on a beach and followed a path over scrubby indigenous growth out to a headland—loads of little coves, extraordinary birds, and very rare flowers—we went for 1½ hours and didn't see a soul. It was really breathtaking. Also some lovely rock pool exploring.

21

Incarnate God

DURING THOSE RESTLESS DAYS, knowing we would move but not knowing when or where, with riots, disappearances, and power outages, I was given an epiphany, a revelation. I'd been looking for god in the wrong places—experiences of victory and guidance, but instead I was shown a god who couldn't be rationalized, objectified, and put into outline form. Berkhof's *Systematic Theology* hadn't prepared me for this.

Like my conversion in 1970, this god surprised me. Typical of god to bring this vision in human flesh, when Lizzy came into my life.

✧

I open the front door and am dismayed to see a black woman with a baby on her back. Someone else who needs me. But with a kind of dignity she explains her situation. She and her one-year-old Nzuzo have been living in servant's quarters a few blocks away. New government rules have been imposed on people who allow their servants' quarters to be used by domestics who are not full time "live ins" for them. Lizzy has been sent packing. "I have heard that you might have a room for us." "Please," she adds, and I'm caught by her voice: that one word somehow underlines our common humanity.

I look at her. "Yes." I'm not going to ask E, since I've heard that the fines are like the price of a house. I don't care.

"Let me show you." She picks up two small bundles she'd put to one side of the door and follows me through the hall, the kitchen, the scullery, across the yard to the outside room. I unlock the door and Lizzy looks inside at the bare walls, bulb hanging down, the bed and nightstand and rickety chest of drawers. She turns to me, tearing up. She takes Nzuzo off her back and puts him on the bed.

"I'm just finishing some soup for supper. Will you come in and eat with me? Or would you rather I bring you some here?" She sits on the bed. "I will come," she says.

Lizzy and I are the same age. She uses our kitchen to cook and we share food with each other. She tells me about her twelve-year-old son Michael who is in the Transkei with her mother, how she sees him every two years when she can afford bus fare.

Lizzy likes to come in and babysit for us in the evenings. We come home from a church meeting and Nzuzo is asleep on the couch, Lizzy ironing. "You don't need to do that, Lizzy."

"You take a risk for me . . ." she smiles.

One day Lizzy gives me a brand-new baby outfit from the South African equivalent of Marks and Spencer, known for their high quality and their easy exchanges. Someone has given it to her, but it is too small for Nzuzo. "I give this to you," she says.

"Oh, but Lizzy . . . you could exchange this! You should take it in and get something for Nzuzo."

"My heart wants to give it to you."

I close my mouth. Lizzy has begun to show me a new god, who cares less about money, and more about kindness and care.

"Thank you," I say.

Aerogram—July 29, 1981

Did you see the Royal Wedding? Everything ceased here while we watched. Though the music had to be dubbed . . . We went to the Bromleys to watch, which was quite an experience in itself. (They're Sir and Lady Bromley) so they had comments about all the people and guards and palace and had cousins and friends there. "Oh look, there's so and so!" etc. Afterwards, lunchtime, they opened some champagne and we had smoked salmon, caviar, and champagne! We drank a toast to the prince and princess and A held his glass up and then drained it! Anyhow it was a bright spot!

OMG

Aerogram—November 13, 1981

We've been very busy—all our usual frantic activity and Christmas coming! We also had a staff conference at Betty's Bay on Monday-Thursday of this week—it was lovely. Anne and I cycled from Gordon's Bay along the coast to Betty's bay—about 40 km—it was lovely—We saw baboons and mongoose (mongeese?) on the way there and while there, besides the meetings, we hiked and swam in the lake and river and walked on the beach. Found a new botanical reserve area with several altogether new kinds of proteas that I've never seen before. On the Thursday we looked out, we saw a whole school of dolphins just 5-10 feet off the shore swimming up and down and jumping. E said there were probably whales there. I was so glad that we had our binocs— we saw two sperm whale out in the bay—say 30 feet from shore—watched them for several hours-tails as big as a boat.

✢

Several months later, I find out I'm pregnant, and I see Lizzy coming into the yard, Nzuzo on her back. She'd been cleaning for someone all day and he weighs at least thirty pounds. "Lizzy, Lizzy, guess what? We're expecting a baby!" She looks up at me and smiles. "I am glad for you."

This doesn't seem quite enough. Everyone else I've told is giddy.

I look at her face. "Lizzy, did you feel that way when you knew you would have Nzuzo?"

She smiles at me again. "I did not need this baby," she says.

What? I know how much she loves him.

But her life is hard.

I am a child excited about a new doll.

She smiles at my puzzled face and pats my arm. "I am glad for you."

Lizzy holds contradictions: she loves her baby but obviously didn't plan on this pregnancy. She carries the burden of motherhood—not just metaphorically with worry and protectiveness, but physically as she has Nzuzo wrapped onto her back traveling and working every day. She gives even though she is poor. We're physically the same age, but spiritually she is way beyond me.

I go out one evening to ask Lizzy if she can babysit. I tap on her door and hear muffled sobs.

I open the door: she sits on the bed, clutching Nzuzo, rocking back and forth. "The man . . . at government office when I go to get my pass fixed up . . . he say I can't keep Nzuzo . . ." She rocks and cries.

"What?!" I am outraged. "How can they say that?! I'd like to get my hands on them . . ."

Lizzy continues rocking and crying for five minutes. "We can't let this happen," I hiss.

Her voice, rocking, very soft, "God is good . . ." Rocking. "God is good . . ."

I stand stunned. I was the vicar's wife, after all, with strong faith, for heaven's sake. But it would not have crossed my mind to say at a moment like this: "God is good."

I sit next to her; put my arm around her. "Lizzy, I'll see what we can do." She continues rocking, "God is good . . ."

22

A God Who Goes Deep

WHAT KIND OF FAITH is this? How can someone be sobbing, heartbroken, and yet affirming god's presence? Could god be good without being magical?

Lizzy knows something I am just beginning to reach for about god. She has offered me god with skin on. Less magical, more enfleshed, this god chooses vulnerability, invites us to knit our sufferings into the sufferings of Christ.

How could I have missed that god for so long, central as this weak god is to our faith and the church year? Not the triumphant ride into Jerusalem nor crowds thronging to hang on his words: we glimpse god most clearly in the garden. Jesus prays, sweating blood in his ordeal, "Let this cup pass." We have no idea how long it took for him to get to, "Thy will, not mine, be done."[1] Maybe hours. But even Christ could not take the shortcut, sidestepping the agony, sweat, tears.

In Lizzy's Gethsemane, in mine, in yours—when we feel we have lost what matters most, when friends don't understand, when our way of looking at the world teeters—that is where we enter the Christian narrative most fully.

I am catching a glimpse of this great truth we visit week by week in the Eucharist—as even Jesus has to retell the old story.

At that Passover table, Christ makes a cosmic paradigm shift, which echoes down the ages, rattling the chalices on our altars today. Not simply reciting the Passover story again this year, Jesus brings his fear and angst and weaves it onto the warp of Passover deliverance, thereby creating new

1. Luke 22:41–42.

meaning. In his retelling, Jesus moves himself and his followers from one vision—Messiah leading cheering crowds to victory over the Romans—to some unknown (probably painful but authentic) future. The old story emboldens Christ to say "yes" to the unimaginable, and a table is spread for the feeding of future generations.

At that Passover, Jesus, real flesh and blood, is confused, scared. Dust, laughter, sun on shoulder, tears—life would soon be gone. People who had baited and bullied him. Some who wanted to follow but were so weak. Sore feet, aching hunger, exhaustion. How would he handle torture? Where were the promises?

Sitting with friends for this Passover meal, the familiar story comforts: people enslaved, brutalized, making bricks in the heat, endless whippings. The bread: wheat ground between huge stones, olives crushed, water hauled under straining muscles. In the incarnation god chooses the limits of flesh: this is my body. Human sweat and earth-rooted harvest, all enfleshed in this bread that rests in these hands, torn fingernail, childhood scar. Looking at the bread, telling the old story: Jesus rips it apart. "This is my body," Jesus says. "Broken. For you. For everyone . . . Don't forget."

And the cup of blessing. How many Passovers had he poured and drunk that cup? But this time—baskets of grapes lugged and crushed, the utter bloodiness of the wine. Blood dripping on doorposts, blood of children dying, his own blood. "My blood. Poured out." His fear sounds the depths of the old story. "A new promise, a new way of knowing God. Here. Now." Jesus' veined, soon-to-be-bloody hands lift the pottery cup.[2]

The Passover story was meant to be one of deliverance—a magical god's power to bring plagues, to hold back the sea. Jesus retells it as a story of weakness, vulnerability, flesh—one who does not magically deliver. This story begins with Jesus' birth, not in a Hallmark card kind of barn, but one in which birth is a bloody mess and animals produce real manure.

Presumably—with his connections—Jesus could have chosen otherwise—rather not get my hands dirty, thanks anyhow, my heart broken. No bleeding for me . . . I'd rather look like my Sunday school portraits—meek, mild, holding only the whitest of lambs, the cleanest of little white children in their pastel Sunday best.

God's full presence in flesh and blood—the incarnation sets a pattern. We are not pulled out of flesh: This is my body. In it I feel a baby's warm skin against mine. This is my body: delight, hunger, weariness, aging, disease.

2. Luke 14:14–22.

We were never meant to be schizoid, moving from our brokenness to pristine host, like going through airport security, relinquishing reality before we board the altar steps. What we need is one who will enter pain with us, hear us out, help us come to a place of grace.

Lizzy is showing me this god. I sit with her, holding her as she rocks, "God is good."

Knowing powerful white people, we are able to pull strings, so she can keep Nzuzo with her. But that is not the real story—the real heroism, the sainthood, the real story is her rocking: "God is good . . ."

The god Lizzy has shown me opens me to deep human emotion, to presence in the given moment, to holding it all in god. But I have no idea how to do that: the god I've known up till now asks me to ignore my emotions, to assume they are leading me astray. I will have to learn to live with a god who has chosen vulnerability and involvement, who is present in times of despair and joy.

✧

After months of waiting, the church in St. Paul phones and asks us to fly over the next weekend for an interview. Six months pregnant and huge in my calico jumper, I fly first class since the tickets were bought so late.

On the plane, the Lord gives me a verse—"they shall come from the east"—so I knew we are called to St. Paul.

When we are back in Cape Town, the search committee phones and invites us to come.

In the midst of loading a container, Susannah is born.

Her birth overwhelms me:

"I cried and cried."

"Why did you cry?"

"Because I was so happy. Two boys and now a girl."

For thirty some years now, I tell her the story. After hours of labor: dark, curly hair pressed hard against this head, and one more push and she slipped out—a girl, and I wept and held her against my breast and wept. Hello. Welcome. Hello. This is my body. This is your body.

For years I didn't tell her about her beginnings: Conceived, skinny-dipping under the Southern Cross, naked flesh smoothed against naked flesh; delight in dark velvet water, joy under a sensuous February sky. No drugged, sleepwalking duty, this—I was awake to nakedness and delight.

No elegant silks, filmy lingerie, artful annunciations, but sand, passion, moon, water—primal elements of the universe. No veil protecting sperm from egg. Flesh: and there she was.

I couldn't have known it at the time, but in her I conceived much more than I bargained for. That's true with all babies, I suppose, but she forced her way into the world, making me mother to a daughter, pushing me until I had to face what it was to be daughter to a motherless mother. She forced my hand, my mind, my soul, bringing me face to face with rage, forcing me to grapple with the dark legacy of fear, and those dark waters became a healing spring—charming me under a starry sky in a South African lake.

Little one, conceived in a lake—she hated being prone, helpless. When I laid her body across mine to nurse her, expecting her soulful eyes to stare into mine, warm milk dripping from the corner of her mouth, she twisted from me, pulled herself upright, so she could see the world. This is your body.

At her birth, I wanted someone who would be closer than close, like-minded as I never could be with Andrew and Stephen. Some primal urge of mine wanted her to be sweet and dependent, to stare lovingly at me with long-lashed eyes, bake cookies and bread, sit and listen to stories.

Yes, I cried and cried when Susannah was born. Wide-eyed and somber in my arms on the delivery table, she had already the eyes of a wise woman who would push me kicking and screaming from a narrow comfort into a broader place, reborn as I gave birth.

Once again, I was overwhelmed by the primal call of motherhood, changing a person from the inside out. Heart-wrenching pictures show women during war-time awaiting news of their sons; mothers whose children are torn from them; mothers cradling the bodies of their little ones. In war and peace, the experience of motherhood is raw, filled with intense love, overwhelming fear, ferocious protection. My strongest calling was to protect my family. Or was it? What would Lizzie say?

And she was a girl! I knew enough of the pressures to be sweet and nice. And as a Christian didn't I know what god wanted of women? Can a girl be raised without being taught how to bow to men's needs, how to curb their emotions?

23

A God Who Invites All Emotion

I NEED MY SIMPLE god as we prepare to leave South Africa. I nurse Susannah as I sit with people in our living room, telling them the story. The phone call, the prayer on both ends. God "giving me" verses about bringing us home from being scattered afar. Their prayers that someone would come and bring new life to their parish and the church in Minnesota. It is so clear. Our leaving must be miraculous to make it possible to bear the good-byes, people sitting in the lounge at Christ Church House as if this is a wake.

E is too busy and distracted to sit with the endless stream of visitors, so I do. I feel people's waves of sorrow, but also my relief: we are climbing into lifeboats and paddling away. And these were mostly white people. In other gatherings coloured people would shake hands fervently with me. Good-bye, I'll never see you again, and you will probably die in the revolution. Tiny Susannah felt it all and cried inconsolably.

I couldn't begin to allow my emotion to bubble to the surface. Like so many women who are forbidden rage, like my mother who could never express her loss, I had to push my emotions away. As Dorothee Soelle suggests, women have been told to turn down the reality, silence the anger, mute the complaints. They have been expected to simply get over losses, their emotions—over miscarriages, babies wrenched from unwed mothers, boys called up to fight, or daughters married into abuse. Soelle puts it this way: "Perhaps there is no weapon that has been used as perversely and effectively against the otherness of children and women's conscientization than this creeping trivialization of experiences and feelings, that are considered pointless for the struggle for survival."[1] The tears of the "little woman,"

1. Soelle, *The Silent Cry*, 13.

the "just get over it," belittle the passion of motherhood as it echoes the passion in the heart of god.

This trivialization leads to a "good girl" mentality, a need to get it right on the outside. How can you live with a god who wants you to be both authentic and nice?

I'd learned from childhood that only sweet feelings were to be owned. All others were to be deeply buried.

I grasped how profoundly I had learned to submerge feelings on an early July morning in 2004. My mother's voice drops to a whisper, although we are alone in the house together. "You must never tell anybody," she says. "Not a soul."

I can't imagine what mom plans to tell me. That I am adopted? That she was a victim of incest? That my father was secretly gay?

"My grandfather had an affair," she whispers. "I didn't know until my grandmother was dying. She was there on her death bed—stomach cancer you know—and she really wanted to tell me something. So I leaned in very close to her and she told me that my grandfather had an affair. You mustn't tell anyone."

I'm tempted to smile. This would have been over a hundred years ago, and still a secret.

"Do you know who it was with?" I ask. Has this come up because this is the first time I've seen my mother since my husband had an affair and decided on a divorce?

Her voice drops even lower. "Yes. It was her sister."

My namesake Mary Ellen and her sister. I wince. I thought a close friend was bad enough.

"That's awful," I say.

"They patched it up, though," she quickly reassures me, ratcheting up the volume on her voice. "That's why I never knew about it. They worked it out." What does "working it out" mean? Living with rage until it turns to stomach cancer?

"I don't know why she wanted to tell me," my mom shakes her head. "It was like she needed to tell someone before she died. But remember, you must never tell anyone." My mother was likely the only person my great grandmother told, and I was the only one my mother told.

I nod. My great grandfather Kent's affair with my great grandmother's sister must have happened in about 1890. Why is this such a deep, dark secret that I mustn't whisper to a soul, one my mother never told anyone, that her grandmother never spoke until she spent her last dying breath on it?

My great grandmother Mary Ellen, my grandmother Anna, my mother Grace and me—we are all part of the cult of married women, initiated into the terrible mysteries of lust and intercourse. We know what men are like—animals really, who need placating, to be handled carefully or they will go off with another, and that's just their nature so no one can blame them . . .

Those pictures of that very proper Victorian family—my namesake great-grandmother Mary Ellen, sitting with her stiff starched clothes and collar buttoned up, her hair heaped on her head; she stares at the camera, told by her whole society to be serious, stiff, still. Now I understand the pain in her eyes.

Next to her is my great grandfather Kent, with his large moustache, the picture of propriety as he stands, short, stocky in his waistcoat and pocket watch, staring grimly into the camera. The upstanding community member. Who screwed his wife's sister.

What is the correct response to your husband having an affair with your sister or a close friend? To someone you love betraying you or being betrayed? What is the correct response to lies covering adultery? The appropriate response to cruelty and oppression?

Rage was literally unthinkable to my great grandmother, grandmother, mother, and most women down the ages. Instead of rage—helpless anxiety. Rage might have delivered them from years of sleepwalking depression and bitterness.

My reliance on this rational man—our common values, our vows, our god—how was this different from that woman who was my great grandmother—who stared stiff and still at the camera? We were both trying to hold our worlds together.

⌖

When I told Lizzy we were moving to America she teared up. Others might say they would try to come and visit, but for Lizzy that was impossible. Fifteen years later I got a letter from someone, inviting many of us who had known and loved Lizzy to contribute to buying her a house in Transkei. I sent $500.00. But I am still vastly in her debt.

And I learned about some unintended consequences.

In those few months before we leave, I start getting phone calls:

"Mrs. Ashcroft?"

"Yes."

"I'm desperate for domestic help. Interviewed a girl called Mable. Did things go missing while she worked for you?"

"No. She was very honest."

"Do I detect an accent?"

"Yes, I'm American."

"Oh, I see. I have the feeling that Mable is well . . . cheeky . . . but that wouldn't bother you. She tried to tell me that you paid her the most enormous salary, but natives are so bad with numbers."

"We paid her eight rands a day."

"I hope you realize you've spoiled her."

No, I didn't realize, I thought. I still felt mainly relieved to have her out of my life. Was my experiment, trying to assuage my guilt, complete self-indulgence?

Just before we moved, Mable came to visit.

"How are you? Are you working?" I ask.

She shakes her head. "No good job yet."

"I'm sorry." I mean it. My experiment disappointed me but harmed her.

"I hear you move to America. Before you go I want to show you my new man-child." Mable swings him around and holds him facing me. Hair kinky black, dark, dark skin, just like his brothers and sisters.

"Wait," says Mable. "Wait till he opens his eyes. He has Andrew's eyes."

I can't even say "what?" before he opens his eyes. They are green.

His parents and his siblings all have dark brown eyes. E and Steve have blue eyes. But this baby has green eyes like Andrew and me.

"That's because he was made during the months I was working at your house," Mable explains. "I played with Andrew and talked to him and this one got his eyes."

I look at Mable, at the baby, and back at Mable. I open my mouth. I close it, swallowing my exposition on how somewhere back in her or her husband's genetic pool there must have been a forebear with green eyes. Neat, rational explanations, easy answers, don't add up here. Or anywhere.

I look into those green eyes and wonder what they will see as they grow up, as I've been forced to, in South Africa.

PART SIX

24

A God Who Thickens the Plot

YES, I WAS BEGINNING to grow up. But I still needed a god who yanked our marionettes off a South African stage and plunked us down onto a Minnesota one. Moving continents with two toddlers and a baby, I needed a god who would pull the strings, so I could dance. For years, when asked about our move, I would tell the spiritual story about the call, the Bible verses, the need of the Episcopal Church in Minnesota. I was unable to take responsibility for the choice to leave a terrifying country.

⌁

Though we were miraculously called, the move from high summer in Cape Town to frigid winter in St. Paul, was not the smartest. A long flight to Amsterdam and a night in a hotel. We walked along a canal, temperatures in the forties, and Steve and Andrew wail, "It won't be this cold in Minnesota, will it?" No. Not exactly this cold in January in Minnesota.

Then the flight to Minneapolis/St. Paul and fifty people from the church, bearing coats, hats, mittens. "We want to see snow!" The boys run outside and touch a huge plowed drift. "Snow is cold!" they run back to report.

The church, defying the bishop who wanted to hire local, bought us things they could see we needed when they unpacked our container into the house they'd rented for us. We were welcomed.

But daily, E took our one car to the church some three miles away. Four-foot snowbanks blocked sidewalks, so a stroller couldn't fit through.

I was stranded with three kids . . . one sobbing for his best friend Tim, one having tantrums, and one screaming with colic.

And the church! We're used to lively worship, friendly faces, big crowds. E preaches thirty to forty minutes when people are used to ten. "Sermon-ettes make Christian-ettes," he responds to complaints. The music program falls apart. I do post mortems after services to figure out what could have been better. After all, I'm his helpmeet. Or at least his cleanup crew. He becomes defensive. Over the next year, many people leave the church.

Is this what church is like without the benefit of pending revolution?

Everyone assumed we were glad to be out of the pressure cooker of South Africa. And we were, but everything seemed so fuzzy. In apartheid South Africa, good and evil were clear. In Minnesota it seemed that "anything goes" was the motto.

I clung to my evangelical, magical god, because I assumed that the alternative was this open-minded relativist one. It took me years to recognize that the Judeo Christian god is neither one where all is black and white, nor a liberal, "hey, whatever" god. Dorothee Soelle writes about the ubiquity of this laissez-faire god in Nazi Germany: people in liberal churches assuming it was fine for them to go to concerts while death camp-bound freight cars rattled by. But as Soelle says, this kind of passive tolerance is the opposite of love in its apathy and laziness.[1]

This broad-minded god appeals: he only wants us to be happy, to follow our own desires. This ethos is so prevalent we may forget it is the new kid on the block. One of the biggest shifts in the last hundred years, argues James Davison Hunter, in his book, *Death of Character*, has been our societal move from honoring character—affirming faithfulness and truth telling, while rejecting instant gratification, betrayal, and family abandonment—to the exaltation of personal satisfaction. As a profession, psychology has taken over the realm of character development, prioritizing the therapeutic and self-referencing: the center point of this moral framework is the autonomous self.

A motherly god (and the biblical narrative) has little time for this focus on individual happiness and personal fulfillment: what's lost here is tragic—a mature, principled center in which moral character chooses constraint and says "no" to personal appetites for the sake of the greater good. One of the gifts of the biblical narrative is that it portrays what happens

1. Soelle, *Suffering*, 36, 41.

when people "abide by their convictions even in, especially in, the face of temptation or adversity,"[2] and the consequences when they don't. Without this moral center, according to Hunter, we end up at the mercy of other forces, such as consumerism and pop culture, which do not have the depth to guide our lives.

In Minnesota, we are dizzied by our reverse culture shock. Then E is asked to go look at a church in Connecticut, a well-known, evangelical and charismatic Episcopal church. We fly to a wealthy suburb of New York City. The rector, who is an outstanding speaker and pianist, has been traveling so much that the church board has reached a solution: hire an assistant to run things.

E would be hired as a Band Aid: It is crystal clear to me that the church just wants to keep their celebrity rector. After the poverty and sacrifice I've seen in South Africa, plus the hopes of, and cost to, the folks who've worked so hard to bring us to St. Paul, how could we choose this?

We fly back to St. Paul. I'm glad E is head of our household—the strong, objective one, the one who can be depended on to see the will of God.

So it was in June 1985, that the foundation cracked as we sat at the dining room table: "God wants us to move to Connecticut," E says.

The room sways. "But we've been in St. Paul just over two years," I say.

Eleven years before I had made my solemn vow. I take you: for better, for worse. In our fairy-tale he'd been cast as hero—rational, mature, while I played the emotional, changeable woman.

I take you: for richer, for poorer. But this? A new, more glamorous opportunity, and he names it god's will? Not just more prosperous, but something different, some place where he will be admired.

I take you: in sickness, in health. But his mask has slipped, and I see a person carefully hidden—by him? by me?—for all these years. This is not the man I believed him to be. But really terrifying: he is not the man he thinks he is. I take you. Yes. But what if I've woken to find myself in bed with a stranger?

"We're not moving," I say.

Sitting there, I am dizzied. The shaking stops; dust settles, sifting over cracks in my life. I barely catch a glimpse of myself as a compliant, superstitious child, see myself still living out of my childish religion, my belief in

2. Hunter, *The Death of Character*, 16.

some grand design—mumble the right incantations, be meek, and god will do the rest.

The precipice has yawned open and snaps shut. I pull back, spinning with vertigo, "No, let's play house . . . I'm the mommy, you're the daddy." For years I would pretend I hadn't seen the cracks. I could not begin to fathom what my discovery might mean. How could I open my hands and release my childlike life—bills paid, decisions made for which I bear no blame—and grasp responsibility, wisdom?

When I first saw those cracks, I was thirty years old, very mature, I thought. I had no college degree, no sense of vocation, since my work experience was primarily as a minister's wife and a mother of three. I thought of myself as too emotional, too sensitive, to survive in the real world—though I'd managed a large household in what looked like impending revolution South Africa. E was seven years older and had a PhD in bacterial genetics and was wonderfully sensible. What could I give him, poor as I was? It was hard to let go of the idea of needing a daddy who "brought home of the bacon."

E phoned the church in Connecticut to say no, because his wife didn't think it was right. They put an extra $30,000 in the package, assuming that would help his wife feel better about it. We stayed in St. Paul.

I went on building a wonderful childhood for my children—no TV, so many books, private schools, backpacking in the North Cascades, museums in Europe. The narrative served us all. But E's restlessness formed a pattern in our marriage. Every few months he would find a new church and think we were called.

Where was god? I was living the life of a good, supportive wife. For eighteen years after we sat at that dining room table we lived the narrative that held our world together. After all, I had promised. I could live in this safe world and raise my children—I could rescue my husband while he rescued me.

24

Getting Over the Daddy God

THE CRACKS IN MY sense of who E was, and therefore what husbands were meant to be, and thus what men were like—superior and rational and called to lead—began to affect my god image. Born in the fifties, and then into the misogyny of fundamentalism and the traditionalism of the Anglican Church, I had assumed that god was father. This image of god began to weaken in South Africa: there, god as father would have meant god absent, impregnating with some great new thing and then disappearing. Maybe providing some material support, but too busy or absent to listen or be present. But with my ultra-logical man and a church focused on fine preaching and good theology, I'd valued all those certainties over my own way of being that was passionate, intuitive, and fiercely unreasonable in my love and commitment.

This change in god image—from one necessarily HE to one who encompasses the feminine—is one of the most difficult shifts we are called to make in our god growth. One of the divides most fully built into Western society (and particularly Western theology) is the one placing things in two clear columns. On the one hand you have the rational, male, spiritual, exalted, and logical; on the other you have female, flesh, earthy, intuitive, demeaned. Built on Plato, these binary oppositions have thrived throughout the history of the church.[1]

Beginning to see god as mother—in flesh, childbirth, motherhood—women experience the depths and heights of the created order. A good mother not only wants her child's happiness but also her child's growth and strength. The "Old Testament" god who people often see as a mean old man

1. Morley, "I Desire Her with My Whole Heart."

is a motherly god—like a good Jewish mother, this god loves unconditionally, demands good behavior, vocalizes rejection and pain. Being a mother or yearning for a child—these intense longings and loves run through the biblical text, showing us the heart of god.

Only years later did I see how I was running so I wouldn't need to look into the deep contradictions at the heart of my theology. My narrative had expanded and stretched to breaking point. The story bulged and bowed for years. That old idol, who answers all prayers according to his will, "who doesn't let the righteous hunger,"[2] had fatal cracks from years in South Africa, and yet I held on.

❧

Susannah turned two, and E and I decided I should finish my degree. I would become an elementary school teacher: I knew I could do kids. With great fear—could I pass a college class?—I enrolled in a developmental psyche course at nearby St. Kate's, loved and aced it. That fall I took a philosophy course and thought I'd died and gone to heaven. European history, more philosophy, literature—I was standing under a waterfall. For my major I needed thirty hours of classroom experience. I asked a favorite teacher at my kids' school and visited her class. Within an hour I was bored and irritated.

I took inventories and interviewed people in various jobs—I should become a writer or a college professor. No jobs there. Or a minister—but one in any family was plenty, I said. I changed my major to English, graduated, and began a PhD program at the University of Minnesota.

I loved teaching freshman comp—helping these young people find their voices. I wrote books, collaborated on plays for church, organized house groups. I picked up kids from school and dropped them at opera rehearsals, soccer clubs, hockey practice.

Our narrative stretched and held.

In the summer we took the kids west to be with my parents. On San Juan Island, when the first child stirred, I'd get up and take them for long walks so that my parents wouldn't be disturbed, and E could catch up on sleep. Back in Bellingham I'd plan and outfit a backpacking trip with one child for three to four nights in the North Cascades.

2. Psalm 37:15.

The split I experienced echoed the one that drove me to England in the first place, but I didn't even see it. On the one hand was a god who called me to grow and learn, to teach and write, who invited me to joy in the wilderness. On the other was a god who promised that a family that prays together stays together, who wouldn't let anything bad happen to me.

As I began teaching at Bethel University, I met wonderful women who had decided to come back to finish their degrees. Having married their Christian college sweethearts, they had quit school to have babies. Now their kids had reached a stage so they could finish their degree. Over years, every single one of them ended up divorced. The husband, they tell me, is "so supportive" and is really glad she's passing classes, so she can get a job. These women don't realize that learning and growing may place them in an impossible position, as they feel pulled apart by their awakenings, their vows, their callings, and their lives.

For years I wanted to warn them—the new ones. To say, "you know what you're getting yourself into? Do you know the pain this will cause for you and your children?" But then I think, "No, that's not been true for me. I'm so fortunate to have a husband who is not threatened by my having found and using my gifts."

⊝

E was offered a job in the suburbs. I was distraught about leaving my church community, but god gave me a verse—from Acts about the people of Macedonia appearing to Paul in a vision, "Come over and help us."[3] Oh well, I guess we had to move across the Mississippi River, lo, even to inner ring suburbs to obey the call of god.

And anyway, as a feminist I knew I had my vocation and E had his, so this was his decision. I was writing books, speaking and leading retreats all over the country, teaching at Bethel and Regent College, ferrying children.

I went for the first time into the Boundary Waters Canoe Area Wilderness and met the god of great silences I'd known in the mountains. Water and light and rippling sun on trees: soon I was spending much of my summer in wilderness. The joy of light on lakes, and northern lights fluttering through the sky, filled my soul.

As a college professor, I loved developing courses on literature by women, African literature, narrative theology. I spoke at retreats and

3. Acts 16:9.

conferences—blending word crafting with connecting and focusing on people's real needs. People asked me why I wasn't ordained, and I would raise my eyebrows, "One in any family is enough, I think."

St. Stephen's wanted to hear more women's voices from the pulpit, so I started preaching regularly. We celebrated with friends after my first sermon. I didn't allow myself to see that I was on thin ice here—women were to help, not supplant.

"Mom, why aren't you a priest?" the kids asked, and E agreed, "Yes, I think you should be ordained. Absolutely." After discernment in a committee, at the diocesan level and on my own, I went ahead for ordination.

We talked endlessly about where we would retire and went on holidays to check places out—Dorset, the west coast, the north shore of Lake Superior. But my idea of a great day off was canoeing or snow shoeing, and his was to have lunch at a five-star restaurant where he could chat knowingly with the chef and the sommelier.

Women on canoe trips I led talked about their husbands as wounded performers, out of touch with their feelings, so I assumed this was the norm. E, I told myself, was wounded, oblivious, but good at heart.

He came home despairing of men he'd counseled: "Don't they understand the promises they've made? Can't they see that even if they're not having physical affairs, emotional ones are just as bad? How can they do that? What about their vows?"

Recurring dreams spoke truth: in them E announced he'd sold the house, decided to marry someone else. I told him about these dreams and we laughed together, calling them "E the villain" dreams, carefully framing them as laughable neuroses that I, as the emotional one, brought to our lovely life together.

Our narrative seemed so solid. Six months before E told the children that he was leaving, we had a couple visiting: the wife had early onset dementia. As we watched how her husband cared for her, my daughter said, "You know how Helen's dad looks after her mom? Dad would be like that to you." "I know," I answer. "I hope I would be that to him."

PART SEVEN

26

When the Narrative Fails

IN MANY/MOST/ALL LIVES, A time comes when the narrative fails: it pulls and trembles on the edge of breaking, and then expands again. For years the story can be stretched to incorporate new evidence. Our longing to keep the comforting, oft-told tale and our familiar gods seduce us to turn a blind eye to contradictions and inconsistencies.

But the time comes. No matter how carefully we craft our lives, install security systems, squirrel away rainy-day funds, eat organic food: the plot thickens. Lights begin to swing, floors shake, buildings begin to totter: we realize we are not in control. No wonder trauma is so deeply disorienting. A terrible diagnosis, the death of someone close, the realization of a lie—and you are left amidst the fragments.

Our whole way of being in and understanding our world is called into question. This can happen on a personal/individual level or on a national one, for example with the September 11 attacks or the election of Donald Trump.

Not only does the narrative break; the god holding that narrative together cracks. This god doesn't answer prayers according to his will, doesn't hold together a family who prays together, doesn't give us friends who can be trusted. And the aftershocks shake the past: where was this god when he so clearly called us together and gave us children? And who knows where this god will be in the future?

⊷

We order a glass of wine, dinner. "You've got to tell me what's wrong," I say. "Well, you were right," E says. "B has been attracted to me for some time. We are in love. I want a divorce."

My bowels turn to water. "No one will mind," he says, taking a sip of wine. "The kids really like her." He takes a bite of his salmon. Twenty-nine years of what had seemed to many, and even to me, to be a harmonious, peaceful marriage. She is my friend. He is respected in the community, admired by his children.

This is madness: he stands at cliff's edge. Jumping will devastate our children, injure so many.

"I will protect you," I say, "keep your secret while you get counseling. Only you must promise me you won't see her." He relents, backs off from the plan for an immediate divorce. "Only in staff meetings or at church services," he says. "I swear it."

Over the next four months I imagine him telling our children. I struggle to eat, to sleep. In bed with him at night, I beg god to bring my husband back, and trust god to make it happen. How can this not be god's will?

"Thou shalt not commit adultery." God says, not because it's naughty, but because we are naked and fragile. Great art echoes with the tragedy of the affair, not from prudishness, but because the human psyche needs safety. Adultery, prostitution, incest, rape, are evils because flesh matters.

Overwhelming, complicated pain. This felt worse than death. At this threshold, as he happily ate, there was so much I couldn't see. I run to the bathroom to vomit.

I phone friends in South Africa, in England, begging them to pray for him. We have been the paradigm of a great couple, and they sob when I tell them about his affair as if I'm reporting a death. The god who would protect me, my family, who would answer prayer—that god is put on trial.

Claire phones me with her vision at an ordination in Grahamstown, South Africa. E in a glass pillar and it's as if he cannot see the glass that is holding him in . . . pray for a shattering of the glass.

Could this god pull him back?

I pray frantically, recite psalms, please god, please god. I obsess over the scene of him telling the children. Sometimes in the night as he snores by my side, I find my holy oil, sign him with the sign of the cross, claiming him back as a child of god.

During those most awful months when I was trying to keep his philandering under wraps, I pray and pray—please god, please. Is god deaf?

I thought it was my high-minded commitment to my solemn vows, that I was the virtuous one, trying to hold our marriage together. But mixed with that, I see now, was fear, vertigo. I was not ready for a life without him. I desperately tried to maintain the wonderful, secure childhood and life I'd made for my children.

What was I expecting god to do?

Be the god of fundamentalism? The one who answers every prayer according to his will? That god hears a prayer and checks a file, and says, "Yes, this fits . . . husband stays with family . . . people are not hurt by his walking away from his vows . . . force him back to her. Right, I'll get on this immediately."

I hoped there was still enough magic in this god to wake E up. But what kind of god would force someone to do what they chose not to? That's the kind of miracle even god can't perform, out of respect for human freedom.

Or was I open to god changing me, so that I didn't worry about spending hundreds of dollars on fine wines and gourmet foods? Was I open to god forcing me to do the hard work of creating intimacy where there was none?

E refused marriage counseling. In late December I found out he'd still been seeing her during those horrible months.

27

Telling the Long, Complicated Story

WHEN WE CALLED THE kids to that fateful family meeting, they wondered if maybe their sister was pregnant, or I had cancer. No one would have believed that their strong, stable father was breaking up the family.

My narrative had stretched for many years. But when it broke, I had to process in a wholly different way, asking deep questions about identity, complicity, childhood baggage, chosen and unchosen blindness. These before I could even begin to ask, "What now?"

When a person experiences a trauma, they are counseled to tell the story. The car accident, the surgery, the diagnosis, the adultery, the death of a loved one: telling the story (over and over again) removes some of the shock, shapes the experience, frames it to be not quite so overwhelming. In our own life narratives, we tell the story, revisiting the suffering and loss, to find identity again.

Superficial telling may be therapeutic, but it can also be simplistic, merely whamming in a few additions to the original form. If I shape the story too small, I may freeze it into a fairy-tale, with just a few character shifts—perhaps instead of the princess living happily ever after, I become the wronged victim.

The telling must be done with care, to honor complexity of character. My expectations, needs, and understandings of god come into the mix, as well as those of other main characters. A simple story—in which I am good, while they are bad—could become so real to me through telling and retelling that I begin to forget the more complicated story. If I make the story too small, I do not allow it to become fruitful for me and for those around me.

Telling the story too small, too soon, can push toward a happy ending, a simple resolution: "oh, I see . . . that must be why that happened!" The longing for simplicity moves people to suggest that we claim healing, bow in sweet forgiveness, get over it, and move on: they want to push us into the fairy-tale of neat, sweet endings. Self-help books are the devil's own work, offering the idolatry of easy answers to complex problems, pushing toward quick fixes when there are none. Life's deepest betrayals and losses cannot authentically be dealt with by a reset button. The person whose childhood was taken by an abusive priest, a stunted mother, a violent father; one whose trusted partner or friend betrayed her, a child who disappeared—to "get over" these too easily, to "move on" invites superficiality, pretense, and disintegration. People want you to get over it so they won't have to face your pain and wonder whether this could happen to them.

"Affliction is ridiculous," wrote Simone Weil. She goes on to write about how people want to distance from trauma, to see it as explainable, or as an anomaly, so they can believe it won't happen to them.[1] Onlookers conjure up hasty solutions to avoid the struggle, the exile, the suffering. "Well, she smoked, didn't she?" "They ate processed foods." "Did they eat organic? I didn't think so." "I don't think he went to the doctor much." "Well she was awfully busy . . ." "Did they ever spend much time together?"

A few years ago, I was asked to lead a Lenten retreat for a large church. I offered them a wonderful range of topics: Environment and Spirituality? Women Mystics? They requested Forgiveness.

When I walked into the gathering, where thirty men and women sat, the room pulsed with a palpable longing. I looked around the circle of eager, desperate faces: they expected me to help them to "just get over it."

I dropped my prepared notes to the floor. "What do people say to you?" What followed was a litany—someone spoke, and everyone in the circle nodded and groaned:

"Just get over it."

"Don't let him have the power over you."

"Not forgiving hurts you more than him/her."

"It's been long enough."

"Why would you carry this bitterness?"

"You're only hurting yourself."

"It's like you are ingesting poison and expecting it to kill someone else."

"You seem happy. And he seems happy . . ."

---

1. Weil, *Essential Writings*, 46.

Agony filled the room. A silence.

And then the litany began again:

"And on top of it . . . the religious layer."

"The Lord's Prayer: 'Forgive us our trespasses as we forgive those who trespass against us.'"

"Words of Jesus about what will happen if we don't forgive those who hurt us."

"'Father forgive them,' Jesus said, when they were killing him."

Wow, I thought, looking around this gathering. People don't want to be with you in your rage and pain, they said. They want you to just "forgive and forget," as if it is something you can magically do. As if you are kind of enjoying those feelings of anguish and fury, and you need to give them up as you would chocolate.

The folks at this retreat were all living their individual, complex, painful stories. Not only weighed down by their past trauma, they were pressured to simply move on. They were being counseled (in many ways, by many people) toward the worst possible solution: pretend your pain doesn't exist; tuck your rage away. Hide it so deeply that you think it's gone, where unresolved, it poisons your life. Not dealt with, the skeleton in that closet will not disappear, nor will it simply go away. There's too much meat left on those bones, and it will rot.

The church has made much of South Africa's Truth and Reconciliation Commission. Led by Desmond Tutu, they decided against the blanket amnesty that says, "Hey, let's forget it all happened!" Telling the stories—good parts and bad—gave voice to the teller; they knew they had been heard.[2]

A painful history, according to José Zalaquett (who helped shape South Africa's Truth and Reconciliation Commission) often makes people feel they must choose between truth and justice. Truth must come first, he argues, because, although truth can't bring back the dead, it can release them from silence. If the story is not told, he argues, lies and comforting unreality slip into its vacuum. "Identity is memory," and identities formed out of false stories make people more vulnerable to committing other transgressions.[3]

In a speech accepting the Nobel Prize, Derek Walcott spoke about the breaking of society under colonialism using this metaphor:

2. Tutu, *No Future Without Forgiveness.*
3. Zalaquett, "Truth, Justice and Reconciliation."

Break a vase, and the love that reassembles the fragments is stronger than that love which took its symmetry for granted when it was whole. The glue that fits the pieces is the sealing of the original shape. It is such a love that reassembles our African and Asiatic fragments, the cracked heirlooms whose restorations shows its white scars.[4]

Telling the story doesn't make it all better: it is a painstaking and painful task, involving deep understanding, part of a long process. As Inge De Kok writes: "Large scale restoration of the 'cracked heirloom' is now an established aim of the arts and arts education community in South Africa." It takes time to fix a broken vase, to create art, to tell the story.[5]

The Truth and Reconciliation Commission has made it possible for the country to go on. But twenty years on, many people in South Africa wonder if the TRC pushed them too far, too fast, not allowing deep enough work to deal with all the pain. As we watch the story unfold we may see this is true.

The pain of relationships broken, families shattered, friendships betrayed, can become, like any trauma, a great gift, offering its recipient the chance (the necessity?) of embarking on a demanding pilgrimage. Exhausting switchbacks, mountain peaks, when you would do anything to put the pack down. Just when you reach the summit and think—yes, now it's done! You see the next range looming ahead. We need—not superficial empathy, not analgesia—"never mind! Just be happy,"—not revenge, but a long slow process of working our pain so that it becomes gift. It's not what happens, but how I, how you, how we, as people of faith dig the manure into our lives.

My new god doesn't stand, arms crossed, saying, "Well, has she really forgiven him or not?" In these years of living and writing, I have come to see that forgiveness is vastly bigger and more complicated than the transaction—"do you forgive X?" At the same time, forgiveness is much smaller and simpler—one aspect of who god is and calls us to be. The divine appeal to forgive is one eddy in a swirl of grace, challenge, and encounter.

Just after he told the children: this dream. The kids and I are in a ramshackle wooden house and I see a line of mushroom clouds along the horizon. I frantically put packing tape around windows and watch the tape curl to the floor. I must save my family. I open a door and he looks up, annoyed, from kissing her. I run back to the children, but it is too late.

4. Walcott, *The Antilles*, 4.

5. de Kok, *Cracked Vases and Untidy Seams*.

Stepping bloodied from that womb, I was overwhelmed, dizzy. I didn't believe I could survive. That I would survive. That I wanted to survive . . .

In those black days, I sang over and over:

If thou but trust in God to guide thee
And hope in him through all thy ways.
He'll give thee strength what e'er betide thee
And see thee through the evil days.
Who trusts in God's unchanging love,
Builds on a rock that none can move.[6]

I thought this meant I could trust god to change E, to restore my family. But it turned out to be true in a much deeper way.

Everything was shaken: a sense of success, secure family, financial freedom, a future of travel together, grandchildren, laughing at old jokes. But these are nothing compared to the loss of a god who is good to the good.

When my world was shattered—my sense of what people value, who can be trusted, prayer—fell to pieces. And my god was also shattered. It took years for me to see that god (as C. S. Lewis puts it) as the great iconoclast was the one who was smashed my comfortable, containable god.[7]

Despite my theological understanding and maturity as a person of faith, my gods to this point provided some certainty, predictability, and solidity. The guarantees of a transactional relationship—I'm good and you protect me: was that too much to ask? All those years I'd been following, trying to be obedient, and then everything snatched away like one of those table cloth tricks. (But a botched one, with nothing left intact.) Like the children of Israel, disturbed that their leader has been up the mountain too long, I craved the certainty of an idol.

Terrible emptiness and loss: the god my arms had held onto desperately evaporated. My aching arms, that empty space, and I knew that what they longed to hold could never come again.

What held me? Worship within a tradition familiar and deep. A loving church community. Engaging work. The beauty of the world. None of them filled the void, but they held me back from absolute despair. It's like when you're in the midst of a huge remodeling project and the house burns down.

6. George Neumark (1621–1682); translator Catherine Winkworth (1827–1878).
7. Lewis, *A Grief Observed*.

My narrative and my god could no longer be patched and mended; I had to start from scratch.

Or maybe it just seemed like I was starting over. The love that met me on that May evening in 1970: once the noise of my patching and remodeling—my many words and desperate pleas—faded, I could begin to hear inexplicable love. Like Job I had to get to the end of my pleadings and the explanations of others to begin to hear the voice.

Protection, certainty, success—throw them out along the trail. You won't really miss them. All you need is a glimmerous god.

We all face this challenge: how can we let go of the idol—what we have taken to be god, as St. Augustine put it—and is therefore not god?

Perhaps it was the grace of god that the choice was made for me. That evening at the restaurant that seemed like the yawning jaws of hell, but it has turned into the path to life. That is what god is like. No, I don't believe "It's all good." But I know, "All shall be well."

28

A Glimmerous God

W<small>HAT DO</small> I <small>KNOW</small> of this glimmerous god?

This glimmerous God leaves spaces for freedom, choice, collaboration, creativity; doesn't force belief or compel love. We squirm at relationships where love is coerced, naming it controlling, even abusive.

We may glimpse this god in slow-growing trees, the smell of new baby, Lake Superior tossed and wild. This god glimmers in a thousand places and faces: in the love of friends, in the beauty of nature, the eyes of a great dog.

These glimmers don't compel, they don't even exactly add up, but they become, slowly, artfully, a lovely weaving that inspires, and tends toward belief in a glimmerful, glimmerous God. "Yes, there was something going on there," or "That was pretty amazing. It might have just been a coincidence, but I don't think so." Like the sounds too low for us to hear, the spectrum of light our eyes can't fully see, these glimmers are where this God lives—not in realms of certainty or proofs. As John Henry Newman put it, the cord is stronger than the rod. "An iron rod represents mathematical or strict demonstration; a cable represents moral demonstration, which is an assemblage of probabilities. . . . A man who said, 'I cannot trust a cable, I must have an iron bar' would, *in certain cases*, be irrational and unreasonable."[1] The cord glimmers of god.

My glimmerous god puts things in perspective. I realize my sight is so inherently limited, language so slippery, symbol systems so clumsy— that what I have and can give is the grace and love that my glimmerous god gives me. When I look back, I realize my need to be right was so compelling; now

---

1. Newman, *An Essay,* 199.

I cannot imagine what that was like. Up the mountains, in a cloud—this god brings back words no one fully understands, and that's okay.

The glimmerous god shows me what cannot be shaken, and that is this god's presence, love, and calling. Grandchildren, the beauty of nature, the strength of a church community—I could not ask for more.

Knowing what I know now about this glimmerous god's lack of guarantees, what choices might I have made at key thresholds in my life?

When I first arrived in England, I felt I was on quicksand of a world too old, too deep, too fraught with freedom. Had I known the future, known that a glimmerous god promised no easy path, no "I'm-good-and-you-look-after-me" bargain—would I have been able to step forward?

I travel back to that first morning in England. Standing at the window, looking out over an alien landscape, bells clanging over rows of chimneys, I see it's just as well my magical god didn't offer to share those powers with me. If I'd had them, my life would have been completely different: I would have clicked my heels together and soared back to my pale green bedroom on Cliffside Drive, the desk made from a small door by my dad, a few shelves above with pictures of the San Juan islands, worn copies of *Little Women, The Golden Treasury of Poetry*, a Hummel figurine of two girls singing, given to me by my great aunt. The comfort of those familiars, the sound of gulls overhead and the train whistling between Everett and Vancouver several times a day.

Had I been able to see the future, what would I have done? Could I have flung myself into this life, knowing the pain ahead? The glimmerous god must have held me or I might have withdrawn to live ever after on that narrow slice between Puget Sound and the Cascade mountains.

That window stood open, and I had been pulled to this place by the boy sopranos of King's College. It would be years before I realized that this liturgy, this chapel, this choir, this music, this tradition, had flourished by sucking sweat and blood from the working classes and the colonized of England's great empire.

The beating heart of sung evensong is the Magnificat, the song of Mary,[2] so oft sung there are hundreds of settings, rendered by those piping cherubs. For hundreds of years, pure little boys were the only ones allowed to echo the song of a pregnant Mary, because women were too earthy, too bloody, too emotional, too passionate to approach the altar. When I first heard those piping boy sopranos, I didn't know that they were pressed into

2. Luke 1:46–55.

service, singing the words of a pregnant Mary because the church had followed Plato rather than Jesus. The blood of Christian thought was sucked
out over many years—Jewish earthiness and the incarnation replaced by
Greek dualities. And even in 1973, the closest I could come to the altar was
as a vicar's wife.

Not humble, meek passivity—the "whatever you say, sir" we've been
taught was Mary's response, but the real presence of meaning made within
life, of life, as she said (and we echo) "Be it unto me,"[3] to a vulnerable, motherly, glimmerous god.

So much she didn't know, and yet at that threshold, expectant Mary
sang her song:

> My soul magnifies the Lord:
>
> and my spirit rejoices in God my Savior.
>
> For he has regarded the lowliness of his hand-maiden:
>
> For behold all generations shall call me blessed,
>
> For God has magnified me, and holy is his Name.
>
> He has shown strength with his arm,
>
> he has scattered the proud in the imagination of their hearts.
>
> He hath put down the mighty from their seat,
>
> and hath exalted the humble and meek.
>
> He hath filled the hungry with good things,
>
> And the rich he hath sent empty away.

Listening to the Magnificat (especially sung by boy sopranos) you
might think Mary got it wrong: hundreds of years later the rich, the proud,
and the mighty still seem to be doing pretty well at the expense of women,
the humble and meek, the oppressed. When Mary sang her Magnificat,

3. Luke 1:38.

she had no idea what she had gotten herself into—where her choice at this threshold would lead. No bells warned her that she would live her life as an outsider, no tolling (only thirty-three strokes) gonged painful loss. Like all of us, she was blind to so much. But somehow her sight arced toward a distant ideal, beyond the curve of the earth. Like other visionaries, the near pain fades in the gleam of some greater good, some beauty blossoming out of a yes to a collaborative god. Giving in to the pain and death would open doors—as they have so many years later for me—to freedom and resurrection.

Here I am, the handmaid of the Lord. Be it unto me . . .

What allows us to step through the open door? Ignorance, I suspect. Curiosity, perhaps. Or grace taking voice in a choir singing incarnation—"Of the Father's Love Begotten"—and somehow you find yourself pulled into some cosmic stream, waking to unknown sounds in a strange land. The warning peal those bells sounded faded, and I turned, pulled on some clothes, and emerged into this new world. Be it unto me . . . I said (and say) to my glimmerous god.

Afterword: The Everlasting Arms

In the Magnificat, Mary celebrates her yes to God.

In the Pieta, she holds her dead son on her lap, gazing at his well-beloved features. Over the last three years, that image has intensified for me. In the crucible of my son's cancer diagnosis and death, I have found that within the wrenching sorrow, God's presence holds.

July 17, 2015

I was in Colorado to perform a wedding when the call came. It felt like a lightning strike tearing me from my heart to my bowels. The scar, I think will always be there. "Hey Mom. How are you?" "It's pretty here. The altitude is really something. I'm breathless just climbing the stairs." "Mom, I went to the doctor and they found a large mass in my colon. And then they did a scan and found spots on my lungs and liver." The fire burns and then turns to ice. "Oh, Steve. Oh, honey. You must be scared." "I had a chance to think. I'm most concerned for Anna and Henry and Alice." "Oh, honey I love you so much . . ." "I love you too, Mama . . ."

Those first few months blur. I'd just finished writing *OMG*, and had grappled through to a god who gives us not presents, but presence; not guarantees, but glimmers. At some level I knew "it was well with my soul," but my emotions and my gut lagged behind.

I found myself wishing for a magical god: I wanted to twist god's arm, "naming and claiming" in prayer. I asked everyone to pray for Steve. I knit him a sweater, praying with each stitch. I prayed every way I knew how.

And ways I'd never prayed before. On a shortened sabbatical, I walked into cathedrals and lit candles in front of Mary. For the first time, I could see why people love her: she gets it. She knows what it is to lose a son. Her heart broke as she held his lifeless body. Her encounters with Jesus in the Gospels show a mom who is trying to let her son live his life, while really, she just wants to protect him: agony papered with a smile; aching to hover but walking away.

I light candles for Steve. Mary, heal my little boy. Jesus, heal my little boy. God, please. In the candles, my prayers become incarnate, more than desperate breaths: the clink of coins echoes through stone arches, wicks flicker into flame, wax sputters. Superstition? A year ago, I would have said yes. But how weak we are, how weak I am: bent double by fear and hunger to protect, where else can I go?

In Paris's Sacre Coeur, I watch women in front of Mary: their faces— they've lost a son, maybe have a daughter on drugs, relatives in Syria. I light a candle. Empty ritual, or maybe a sensible humility in the face of an inscrutable universe. Mary comprehends a mother's heartbreak, echoing the heartbreak of Jesus, and the pain of the universe, that "self-same aching, deep within the heart of God" (Rees, Timothy, 1874–1959). Lighting candles to her is an act born of angst. But it is also an act of defiance, declaring my limited understanding. What good is a neat theology that tries to explain everything? I light this particular candle—expressing my mother love in this beeswax—before Mary who understands, and it flames with real presence.

I pray urgently, even though I don't believe that a certain quota of prayers will change god's mind, like one of those games at fairs where you hammer and, with enough umph, the weight rises to ring the bell. As if God has dozed off—all that's going on in the world wears him out—his long white beard gently rising and falling, and our prayers reach a critical mass, raise the alarm, and he drowsily sits up and glances around, "hmm, humph, what's this? Oh . . . lots of people praying about . . . who's this . . . Steve Ashcroft? Well . . . hmmmm . . . cancer, you say? And a young family? Well I'll be darned . . ."

No, I don't believe in that god. But where is god in a terrible diagnosis? When the only explanation is "dumb luck"? When he has a young wife, a three-year-old, and a tiny baby?

God is . . . present. Not accounted for. It seems so unfair.

But why do I expect fairness? Not fair: Here's what my dear Steve said at a gathering with friends and their families a couple of months before he died. A grandpa said, "When I was diagnosed with Parkinson's Disease at fifty-four I thought, this is not fair. You must think that." "Yeah," Steve replied. "But then, I realized I don't apply that standard to good things . . .

like why am I so fortunate to have these great kids, great friends? Do you ask why you are so lucky as to have this lovely granddaughter?"

No, it's not fair that I was born in the United States rather than in Aleppo, Syria or Mogadishu, Somalia. It's not fair that I was born white middle class rather than poor black. It's not fair that I was born in 1952 rather than 1592 or 1259.

When I feel desperate to understand, it helps me to reflect on my limited perspective. Maybe I'm like my Golden Retriever, Sophie, who (although a fine dog) will not and cannot discuss *Hamlet* with me. She's inherently limited, just as I am. Forget *Hamlet*, Sophie. You'll never understand it. But you can sit on the sofa with your head in my lap, and run through the woods with me, finding joy where you can.

I remember god's only guarantee is presence.

When I was working with college students, the one, great taboo was "cheesiness." You could be anything but cutesy or sappy. For years, I avoided that very cheesy poem "Footprints." In "Footprints" the speaker reviews her life with Jesus as if she's following two sets of footprints on a beach. At three or four excruciating periods in her life, she's surprised to see only one set of prints. She complains, "Jesus, why weren't you there in the hardest, the worst times? Why did you abandon me then?" And Jesus replies, "Those were the times when I carried you."

Turns out, that is all we are promised—the carrying, the presence. In some ways, it is helpful to be "acquainted with grief"—my hands had to be peeled, knuckle by knuckle, off my marriage, but also my sense of the way the world is, and the way god is. At some level I assumed that if I was good, god would be good, and keep bad things from happening to me. Being "acquainted" with grief, I knew that God is not a magic Oz behind the curtain, but one who is beyond my ken, and who appears in remarkable glimmers in the beauty of nature, of love, of unexpected moments. God does not add up numbers of prayers for something, check a file to see whether the request fits with his will, and then press an "answer that prayer" button.

Now when I read the "Footprints" poem, I think, "Yes, it's true." I have felt those "everlasting arms" carrying me. This deep peace is a miracle—although not the one I'd hoped for.

We had hoped that some new treatment would come along before Steve died, that a researcher somewhere was working on just the right cure, and that it would come in the nick of time. But if I was just holding onto those hopes—the kind of "hoping against hope" or "naming and claiming it"—I'd be borderline delusional, and that is not faith. Nor is it hope.

I realize that my definition of hope has changed. In those early days after Steve's diagnosis, my hope was frantic: "Please, please, please, please heal him." Not only was it desperate; it was based in the future—Steve's complete healing in some time to come. But during Steve's illness, I came to realize that this moment is all we have. And I have been prone to squander my moments regretting (or wishing for) the past or projecting some unknown future.

If hope is no longer "out there"—something that may happen in some unknown future—what is it? Savoring each moment. Trying to live in the now, which is all I have. Loving as much as I can.

Quality, not quantity. I'm trying to drill down into each day so that it is as full and rich as possible, so that a single day may have more in it than a month carelessly lived. The biblical word for *eternal*, as in "eternal life"—which for most of us carries connotations of long length—in the Greek speaks more of quality rather than quantity.

Maybe it's like memory—when often we think back and remember some things clearly and have forgotten others—how is this like investing in quality rather than quantity? How can I, I ask myself, live so that I'm making great memories—paying full attention to the dew sparkling on our tamarack tree or the veins on a raspberry bush or the feeling of a grandchild's cheek against mine?

✢

Those last days: we didn't want him to die, but we couldn't bear watching weight fall from him, his cheekbones emerging, blood on his teeth in the morning. We didn't want to have to help this big strong man to the toilet. I didn't know how much longer I could hold back my desire to cradle him, stroke his head, to snarl at anyone who came near, "He's my baby . . . get back!!"

As he was dying I saw a split screen—over his big man legs, I saw his pudgy baby legs, crawling on the sand dunes in Betty's Bay, beaming as he felt the fine grains against his fresh flesh.

Tears flowed and flowed. So much love expressed. Why don't we do this all the time? Does it need a death bed scene for our relationships to be exquisite, exotic, and confounding?

That last night Steve's wife Anna slept in bed with Steve. His sister Susannah and friend Chris were there. At one point in the night, the three of them propped him up to give him his medicine, arms around him. Anna said, "It's okay, Steve. It's me and Susannah and Chris, and we love you and we're just going to give you your medicine." Susannah told me he made the little moan he often made when he felt loved and grateful. "Mmmmm . . ." — his last words.

The next morning, I sang through tears, "Lay down, my dear Stephen, lay down and take your rest. I'm gonna lay your head upon your savior's breast. I love you, but Jesus loves you best; I bid you good night, good night, good night. I bid you good night, good night, good night."

In his last moments, he was panting, struggling to get his breath, and I remembered the bed at Mowbray Maternity Hospital in Cape Town, thirty-seven years before: "Mary Ellen, your baby is almost here!" "Go," I whisper to him. "I brought you into this world and now I'm sending you out. Go to be with God."

He pants for a few minutes. "He's gone . . ." Anna says.

⟿

During the last week of his life, I "pieta-ed" my Steve over and over — stroking his face, wiping down his body, singing softly to him, whispering, "I love you so much, Steve." When we say yes to motherhood, we say yes to heartbreak . . . endless letting go. Mary holds her dead son, loving him, but this was the culmination of years of letting go. Some thirty-three years before, she had said, "All generations shall call me blessed . . ." Blessed?

When she said yes, she had no idea what she was letting herself in for. None of us do.

Yes, blessed. I'm blessed by Steve's life and death. By depths of knowing and loving and loss. I don't regret for a moment saying "yes" to Steve's life, this marvelous human being, his relationships, his love.

I'm blessed to know that love is stronger than death. That there are worse things than death. That mysterious and wonderful things happen. That quality is more important than quantity.

I'm blessed to have experienced amazing love and the wonder of God's "everlasting arms." These miracles — love, holding, insight — affirm for me that there's way more to life than meets the eye. Maybe not pearly gates or golden streets, but I'm sure death is not the end.

I believe—not that it's "all good": cruelty is not good. Cancer is not good. And yet, I believe, more strongly than ever, that because God is, "all shall be well."

PART EIGHT

Working it

GOD CALLS US TO reality, integrity, and truth in our inmost beings. Getting there is a lifelong process.

When Jacob wrestled with the angel, he said, "I will not let you go unless you bless me." I said to my trauma: "I will not let you go until you bless me." If I was going to go through this suffering, I was going to demand that it change and deepen me. Telling the story is a way to grasp that blessing.

Telling our stories can help us in this journey toward authenticity. Over these next pages I will pose some questions that helped me along the way, for your own work—by yourself, with a spiritual director, or in a small group.

Workbook

Telling your story #1

Notebook: Take some time to consider some of your major childhood turnings.

1. List five or six major moments or thresholds up to the age of twelve.

2. Take some time to write about these thresholds and how they changed the character that was/is you.

Telling your story #2

People say to me, "I don't believe in god," and I say, "Tell me about the god you don't believe in." The gods we carry from our religious upbringing, from our family life, from earlier stages—have found ways to nestle into corners of our theological backpack, and we may not even be aware that they are there. The process of owning these gods, taking them out of the pack and looking at them, and setting them to one side, begins to make room for a newer, bigger god. This may seem like a long and onerous process, but it is a way that god works. Love woos us; we are not forced nor are our movements like those of a puppet. This god loves us into being and as that happens, other things fall away.

Notebook: Take some time to consider your childhood god images.

1. What kind of gods were you raised with, at home, at church, in your neighborhood? (Remember that, like mine, these god images may be conflicting or multi-layered.)

2. The gods you were raised with—what did they ask of you? (Did you feel you were meant to keep a low profile or to placate or to pray lots?)

3. Were there alternate god images, perhaps introduced by other mentors in your life?

4. How did changes in your life circumstances and character change your sense of the character of god?

Telling your story #3

You continue to shape a growing up story. You are a character, but there are others—including significant romantic partners and fellow workers to parents, siblings, relatives, friends, teachers, etc. And there continue to be major life turnings—things that happen that we must respond to—that become more than story (what happened next?) and reflect plot (why?).

Notebook: Take some time to consider some of your major turnings as an adolescent/young adult.

1. List five or six major moments or thresholds.

2. Take some time to write about these thresholds and how they changed the character that was/is you.

3. Who were some influential people in your life?

Telling your story #4

As we progress through adolescence and young adulthood, our god images change. We also may make commitments that make us feel trapped within certain images.

Notebook: Take some time to consider your adolescent/young adult god images.

1. What kind of gods did you hold on to or let go of, at home, at church, in your neighborhood? (Remember that, like mine, these god images may be conflicting or multi-layered.)

2. These gods—what did they ask of you? (Did you feel you were meant to keep a low profile or to placate or to pray lots?)

3. Were there alternate god images, perhaps introduced by other mentors in your life?

4. Reflect on how the changes in your life circumstances and character also changed your sense of the character of god.

Telling your story #5

As an adult, you make more autonomous decisions.

1. List five or six major moments or thresholds.

2. Take some time to write about these thresholds and how they changed the character that was/is you.

3. What other characters have been central to your adult life?

Telling the story #6

As I was writing this book, I felt as if I began to see myself and others more clearly. This is meant to happen in the telling of our life stories! For me it took the form of seeing how I was complicit or hid from truth: "Oh, I am beginning to see that I had learned to be passive and expect him to be the active one . . ." "Okay, this was not just out of the blue . . . the cracks were there for years."

More profoundly, we may notice patterns. As I was writing this, I began to see a pattern of wanting freedom, getting it, and being terrified by it and giving it up for security.

Notebook: Ponder some of the insights you receive about yourself in the reflecting on/writing about your story.

1. What are some truths you were hiding from, perhaps about your complicity in the events that seemed to be happening to you?

2. What are some indications of the "past, present, and future" of who you are as a character? Of who others are as characters?

3. What are some patterns you see in your life?

Telling the story #7

As we move into mature adulthood, our god images change. You may be in the midst of this journey, having abandoned certain gods, but madly clutching others. And, like me, some life circumstances, when a god has been forcibly removed from you, has probably pushed you to examine your theology—your god images. Like our emigrant or pioneer forebears, we don't usually embark on a journey like this unless we're pretty uncomfortable.

Our sense of god determines not only who we worship and what we expect from life; it delimits our sense of agency. A god who pulls all the strings means I only move lock-step across a stage. A god who invites me to grow up and join the dance asks more of me.

Notebook: Take some time to consider your god images.

1. What kind of gods have you let go of? (Remember that, like mine, these god images may be conflicting or multi-layered.)

2. What are some of the losses as you've let go of this/these gods?

3. What other god images have come to you?

4. What does your new god offer you?

5. What does this god call you to?

Telling the Story #8

Take some time to develop your creedal statement. What is your new God like? List some qualities that have become important to you. "I believe . . ."

Telling the Story #9

How has your story become more complicated as you've told it? What have you learned about yourself and others?

Appendix 1

Metaphors

METAPHORS PLAY A CRUCIAL role in shaping our god images. While the study of metaphors is a huge area, I will provide a brief overview as it relates to growing our god images.

Many of us, if asked what the word *metaphor* means, would answer from our high school English class: a simile without like or as. But really, a metaphor is a way of talking about one thing in terms of another. Metaphors are not just for poetry. Almost all language about abstract concepts, such as love, war, or God, are entirely dependent on metaphor. We use something we know to talk about something that is not as straightforward.

Metaphors are more than words, they are concepts, which have "entailments"—baggage they bring along with them. Metaphors illuminate, but they can also obfuscate. To be a metaphor, there must be both an IS and an IS NOT quality, and it helps if we're aware of them.

Sometimes the IS and IS NOT qualities of metaphors seem obvious—if I say, "My boss is a bear," you don't expect fur, claws, and a propensity to steal picnic baskets.

Sometimes the entailments of a metaphor are less obvious. Take the metaphor "love as madness," well represented in song lyrics—crazy over you, out of my mind over her, etc. We might agree that sometimes love does feel like madness and makes people do weird things, like washing their hair three times a day. Those are the IS qualities of that metaphor—illuminating certain aspects of what young love feels like. On the other hand, the "love as madness" metaphor misses out on the fact that love is hard work and commitment—in these ways, love IS NOT like madness. The metaphor's entailments are misleading.

Metaphors can shape our thinking. "Argument as war" is a conceptual metaphor that Lakoff and Johnson use in their book, *Metaphors We Live By.*[1] They point out all the ways we talk about arguments as if they are war—we win or lose them, we take a side, we cede territory, we take a stand, etc. While illuminating some aspects of argument, the metaphor has so deeply affected our thinking that we struggle to think of argument as other than war. What if we used the metaphor "argument as dance," say? If that metaphor were to become dominant, how would our discussions change?

"Time as money" is another great example. We spend time, save it, invest it, waste it, borrow it, give it, keep it, etc. But many of us have visited cultures that don't live as if "time is money": their attitudes toward money and its relationship with time is very different from ours.

Since all language, and particularly metaphors, are captive to broad, societal values, they can be used (even unwittingly) for ill. In days of early scientific study, a metaphor of nature as a woman being unclothed by science became dominant, and gathered baggage of subjugation and rape, probably affecting our planet today.

Words

Words' meanings change, often reflecting societal changes. Consider the words *icon, interface, gay,* and *twitter,* and how their meanings have shifted in thirty years. Some of these changes are neutral, while others reflect societal biases. For example, the word *whore* originally meant a lover of either sex; *slut* a person negligent about appearance; *wench* a child of either sex; *harlot* someone of either sex. And in terms of overtones, we can see pairings which have changed to reflect societal attitudes: baronet and dame, governor and governess, bachelor and spinster, courtier and courtesan, sir and madam, master and mistress. These changes are called "semantic devaluation"; they explain why it's hard to insult a man without insulting his mother. Language was created within patriarchy, which is not about men vs. women, but about structures built over centuries, mainly by men, often not taking women's lives into account.

Language is like a circle: at the center we stay with the easily intelligible, mundane, and everyday. (One of the challenges when learning a foreign language is that we tend to be stuck in the center of the circle—"Can you direct me to the toilet?"—rather than moving to the edges to discuss

---

1. Lakoff and Johnson, *Metaphors We Live By.*

theology or philosophy.) When we tell jokes, write (or read) poetry, or speak of the abstract, we may be extending the circle.

Metaphors and the Bible

We are entirely dependent on metaphors to speak of god, but metaphors are products (to a large extent) of human culture. We forget that even Moses, when he asks to know god's name, is not given one. God's name is untranslatable without risk of idolatry. We are told in 1 John 4:12 that no one has seen god. Some have argued that the only term for god that is not a metaphor is *holy*.

If we forget god's otherness, or if we lose a metaphor's IS and IS NOT tension, *metaphors can become idolatrous*. Many people's image of god is a cross between the Sistine chapel and a *New Yorker* cartoon.

We need a multiplicity of metaphors for god, and fortunately, Scripture abounds with them—in Psalm 18 alone, god is called strength, rock, fortress, deliverer, refuge, shield, horn, stronghold. In other parts of the Old Testament god is storm, volcano, giant, lamp, judge, general, mad mother bear. Notice that some of these are more culturally embedded than others. We don't see shields all that much nowadays and even shepherds are a rarity. While we have lamps, it's hard for us to relate to a world in which a lamp would make all the difference between utter blackness and illumination. Some of these biblical *metaphors are too distant* for us to appreciate—the IS is too simply too far from our lives.

Worse are *metaphors put to the use of culture*, as some biblical metaphors are over-used while others are ignored. During the Middle Ages, for example, when kings were desperate to consolidate their claims, metaphors of god as king were extremely prevalent, securing greater power for royalty.

Certain metaphors are overused so that, instead of surprising, they underline cultural propensities. Contemporary praise choruses often emphasize our society's extreme individualism, using metaphors that could be summarized as "Jesus is my boyfriend," but mixed up (oddly) with thrones.

Metaphors may become stale and die: "the leg of the table" was probably at one point a remarkable metaphor, like "the leaves of a book." In this case the metaphor has collapsed and doesn't function metaphorically at all.

Metaphors that have collapsed lose their IS and IS NOT tension. This is easier for us to detect with some metaphors than others. There are ways in which god is my rock, in terms of stability, but not in terms of geological history. Some argue that the metaphor of "God is Father" has collapsed as it has ceased to be recognized as a metaphor. Dorothy L. Sayers wrote this about the metaphor of God the Father: "Nor (unless we are very stupid indeed) do we go on to deduce from the analogy that we are to imagine God as being a cruel, careless, or injudicious father such as we may see from time to time in daily life; still less, that *all* the activities of a human father may be attributed to God, such as earning money for the support of the family or demanding the first use of the bathroom in the morning."[2]

Living metaphors always surprise, for in the moment of tension the human imagination discovers that the odd word is more profoundly true than factual description. We see this over and over in the teachings of Jesus as he compares himself to a door, a vine, living water, bread, a mother hen.

Understanding metaphor can move us to a place of greater humility in terms of our sense of god. The sheer multiplicity of biblical metaphors, along with their embeddedness in human culture, will help us to creatively explore our god images.

2. Sayers, *The Mind of the Maker*, 25.

Bibliography

Armstrong, Karen. *A History of God*. New York: Ballentine, 1993.

Augustine of Hippo. *Confessions*. New York: New City, 1997.

The Book of Common Prayer. New York: Church Publishing, 1982.

Brueggemann, Walter. *An Introduction to the Old Testament: Canon and Christianity*. Louisville: Westminster John Knox, 2003.

de Kok, Inge. *Cracked Vases and Untidy Seams: Narrative Structure and Closure in the Truth and Reconciliation Commission and South African Fiction*. In *Current Writing: Text and Reception in Southern Africa*, edited by Meg Samuelson, 5:2, 6 (2011) 76, DOI: 10.1080/1013929X.2003.9678159.

Forster, E. M. *Aspects of the Novel*. New York: Rosetta, 1927.

Friedan, Betty. *The Feminine Mystique*. New York: W. W. Norton and Co., 2001.

Heilbrun, Carolyn. *Writing a Woman's Life*. New York: Ballentine, 1989.

Hunter, James Davison. *Death of Character: Moral Education in an Age Without Good or Evil*. New York: Basic, 2000.

The Hymnal, 1982: service music: according to the use of the Episcopal Church. New York: Church Hymnal, 1985.

Johnson, Luke Timothy. *The Writings of the New Testament*. Minneapolis: Fortress, 1999.

Lakoff, George, and Mark Johnson. *Metaphors We Live By*. Chicago: University of Chicago Press, 1980.

Lewis, C. S. *A Grief Observed*. London: HarperOne, 2001.

———. *Till We Have Faces*. New York: HarperCollins, 1984.

———. *The Voyage of the Dawn Treader*. New York: HarperCollins, 1980.

MacIntyre, Alasdair. "Epistemological Crises, Dramatic Narrative, and the Philosophy of Science." In *Why Narrative?: Readings in Narrative Theology*, edited by Stanley Hauerwas and L. Gregory Jones, 138–57. Grand Rapids: Eerdmans, 1989.

Morley, Janet. "I Desire Her with My Whole Heart." In *Feminist Theology: A Reader*, edited by Ann Loades, 158–63. London: SPCK, 1990.

Newman, John Henry. *An Essay in Aid of a Grammar of Assent*. Notre Dame, IN: University of Notre Dame Press, 1979.

O'Connor, Flannery. *Mystery and Manners*. New York: Farrar, Strauss, and Cudahy, 1962.

Sayers, Dorothy L. *The Mind of the Maker*. New York: HarperCollins, 1987.

Soelle, Dorothee. *The Silent Cry: Mysticism and Resistance*. Minneapolis: Augsburg Fortress, 2001.

———. *Suffering*. Minneapolis: Augsburg Fortress, 1975.

Tutu, Desmond. *No Future Without Forgiveness*. New York: Doubleday, 1997.

Walcott, Derek. *The Antilles: Fragments of Epic Memory: The Nobel Lecture.* New York: Farrar, Straus and Giroux, 1993.

Weil, Simone. *Simone Weil: Essential Writings.* Maryknoll, NY: Orbis, 2006.

Woolf, Virginia. *A Room of One's Own.* San Diego: Harcourt, 1929.

Zalaquett, José. "Truth, Justice and Reconciliation: Lessons for the International Community." In *Comparative Peace Processes in Latin America,* edited by José Zalaquett Daher and Cynthia Arnson, 341–62. Washington, DC: Woodrow Wilson Center/Stanford University Press, 1999.

CPSIA information can be obtained
at www.ICGtesting.com
Printed in the USA
LVHW091624200619
621865LV00005B/848/P